The three authors of *Across the Water* were born and brought up in Dublin and have lived in London since the mid-1970s. Between them they have been involved in the women's and socialist movements in both countries, and in Irish organisations and activities in London. They came together in 1983 to work on this book.

Mary Lennon was born in 1949 and grew up in a working-class family of six. She has been an office worker, a community worker and is currently teaching in a Further Education college in London. Over the past ten years she has been researching the history of Irish women's emigration to Britain and has written articles and given talks on the subject at Irish Studies courses, conferences and women's meetings. She has a young daughter.

Marie McAdam is in her forties and comes from a working-class family. She has worked as a typesetter, an editorial assistant, and taught English in Spain where she lived for a number of years. She has written on Irish culture and politics for both adults and children. She has three sons and is currently a mature student at the Polytechnic of North London.

Joanne O'Brien has a protestant mother and a catholic father. She is a self-taught photographer and a member of Format Photographers, the London-based all-women agency. Her work is mainly portraits and social documentary. She contributed to the photographic book, *Women in Focus* and has exhibited her work in Belfast and London, including her touring show about the cultural life of the Irish in London, *Hearts and Minds – Anam agus Intinn*.

Across the Water

Irish Women's Lives in Britain

MARY LENNON, MARIE McADAM
& JOANNE O'BRIEN

Photographs by Joanne O'Brien

This book is dedicated to all the women who made it possible

Published by VIRAGO PRESS Limited 1988
Centro House, 20–23 Mandela Street, London NW1 0HQ
Copyright © 1988 Mary Lennon, Marie McAdam and Joanne O'Brien
All rights reserved

British Library Cataloguing in Publication Data

A CIP catalogue record for this title is
available from the British Library

Design by Sue Lacey
Printed in Great Britain by St Edmundsbury Press

Contents

Acknowledgements

We would like to thank Claire Keatinge, Ken Lynam, Kevin Simms, and our parents for their help and support while we were working on this book; and our children, Niamh, Joe, Simon, Ruairí and Dónal, for learning to live with endless meetings.

We also wish to thank the following people for their contribution to the book: Marie Ali, Annie Bradley, Veronica Carroll, Mary Cribben, Nancy Dean, Mrs. B. Doona, Kate Duke, Eileen Ennis, Lucy Farr, Pat Finnegan, Beryl Foster, Gabrielle Hamilton, Jane Harper, Fiona Higgins, Nina Hutchinson, Mary Jones, Natalie Kassim, Brid Keenan, Joan Kelly, Venience Kelly, Nuala Keys, Frances Leach, Siobhan Lennon, Mrs. P. Lynam, Phil McAtamney, Bridget McBride, Pat McDonald (R.I.P.), Mary McLaine, Maria McLoughlin, Mary McMahon, Terry McWeeney, Sara Maguire, Madge Messenger, Elizabeth Moore, Nora Murphy, Mary Noonan, Agnes O'Connell, Siobhan O'Donnell, Janice Owens, Maggie Pether, Sue Porter, Bridie Redmond, Colin Robertson, Natasha Sajjad, Jean Somers, Birdie Sweeney (R.I.P.), Caroline Tomiczek, Ann Woods, Bridget Whelan, Nancy White.

Our thanks also to the following groups and organisations: Battersea Arts Centre; Camden Irish Centre; Emerald Butchers; Format Photographers, Irish Women's Centre; London Irish Festival organisers; the National Library of Ireland; Pensioners' Link; the Sheelas Women's Band; and to the Greater London Council Women's Committee for their financial assistance.

The illustration on p. 32 is reproduced by kind permission of the Council of Trustees, National Library of Ireland, and that on p. 35 by London Transport Museum.

For pp. 9, 86, 103, quotations have been used from the following publications respectively: Eavan Boland, 'The Journey' in *The Journey and other poems*, p. 41, Carcanet & Arlen House, Manchester & Dublin, 1986; Eavan Boland, 'Mise Eire' in *The Journey and other poems*, p.11; Sean O'Casey, *Pictures in the Hallway*, Pan, London, 1971.

Introduction

'The silences in which are our beginnings . . .'

We hope this introduction will offer people an insight into how we produced the book and be of use to others who may want to do similar work.

The three of us came together at the beginning wanting to document in some way the wholly unremarked phenomenon of Irish women's emigration to this country. We were all from Ireland, had lived here for between six and ten years, and had known each other a while. We had begun to realize that we were part of the pattern of Irish women's emigration ourselves, despite our different individual reasons for leaving. The discovery that more Irish women than men had emigrated during much of this century and that this was a most untypical pattern amongst immigrant groups moved us to want to learn more. What did this pattern of emigration mean and why were so few people aware of it? There were only a few books available about the subject when we began, but they referred to men's experiences and either totally overlooked that of women or treated it as a minor addition to the main story.

This lack of information about women was reflected on a wider scale by the low public profile of the Irish community in Britain in the late seventies. Cultural and social networks existed, as they had always done, such as Irish dancing, music sessions, the Gaelic Athletic Association, church clubs and welfare organisations, but they were not, in the main, very visible to outsiders. The annual Irish Festival at Roundwood Park in London, where up to 100,000 Irish people gathered, was ignored by the British press, radio and TV. What did exist, we had discovered, were some very negative images of Irish people – violent, stupid, sexually repressed, lascivious and, of course, terrorist. Alternatively, in some circles, romantic images of the Irish were more popular: Celtic, poetic, wild and imaginative – with slightly different variations for men and women. These images also confined and limited us.

In the 1970s such stereotypes gained a new lease of life. There had been an upsurge in anti-Irish racism in Britain as a result of events in the North of Ireland. The fight for civil rights by nationalists in the six Counties meant that the Irish question reared its head daily on TV and in the press. This had its effect on the Irish in Britain and on British people generally. The violent suppression of the civil rights movement leading to an escalation into the present war and the bombing campaign in Britain in the seventies meant that the historical relationship between the two countries couldn't be ignored. A major response from within British society was an upsurge of anti-Irish feeling – from the proliferation of 'jokes' to the distortion and misreporting of events in Northern Ireland, and the process of self-censorship by all major media.[1] The pressures on Irish people, in this situation, to keep a low profile were very strong. Being low key about your nationality and identity was a way of coping with these pressures, as women in the book testify. Political activity by Irish groups in Britain was directly attacked by the introduction of the Prevention of Terrorism Act in 1974. Political activity became dangerous, but even more, the PTA created a climate whereby just being Irish could become grounds for suspicion. The overwhelming majority of Irish people picked up under the PTA have never been charged with any offence.[2]

From the early eighties onwards, the profile of the Irish community began to change, certainly in London where we were based. The deaths of the Hunger Strikers in 1981 had a wide impact on Irish people living here. The time had come, for some, including many second generation Irish, to take a stand. An example had been set by the Black community in resisting assimilation, fighting racism and asserting the validity of their own cultures. The Irish community learnt from this. New organisations were set up to challenge anti-Irish racism. There were pickets of shops, legal cases against newspapers and campaigns against British injustice. There was also a resurgence of interest in exploring Irish history and identity, for example Irish studies, language classes, and conferences. Our book is part of this resurgence and without it, might not have happened. As feminists who had been involved in the women's movement in Ireland and England, our concern was to highlight Irish women's part of the story because of its particular significance in immigration to Britain. Also, just as important, we knew that without our experiences the overall picture is inadequate and distorted.

We approached the Greater London Council Women's Committee with an outline of the book and got funding for two years. The importance of funding to a project like ours, which took five years to research and write, hardly needs elaboration but, crucially, we were able to reduce the time we worked on other things and pay for typing and childcare. It also gave public validation to what we were trying to do. With the abolition of the GLC in the interim, we realize our 'luck' at being in the right place at the right time and the unfair and arbitrary nature of this. Today, it would be so much harder to raise funding.

Finding the Form

Given the resounding silence on the subject, we decided to start with individual women's lifestories and since one of us was a photographer, we envisaged producing a book of photographs and words. This was the approach which appealed to us most. We could then use different women's voices and pictures as strands in the overall story. It was a beginning.

We saw ourselves working in the tradition of books such as oral histories and working-class autobiographies. We very much wanted to produce a book which would be accessible to a wide audience in the way that a photo-text book can be. Photographs often convey experiences which cannot be expressed in other ways and their immediacy is one of their great strengths.

Rather than a statistical survey of Irish women, we wanted to convey Irish women's experiences of immigration as perceived from the inside – in their own words without commentary from us. Through the photographs, we wanted to contribute a permanent visual record of women's lives in Britain. So few images of ourselves are reflected back to us, and generally the perspective is not ours. We decided finally on a book consisting of edited interviews and photographs.

We wanted to make contact with women of different age groups – if possible an age range which spanned this century: women from different parts of Ireland, though with extra emphasis on areas of high emigration; and primarily, working-class women whose experiences are rarely published. In a similar way, lesbian women talk about their varied experiences – an integral part of the story – although they are frequently denied by the Irish community in Britain, as well as facing hostility common in the host community. We also decided to interview women who saw their Irish identity from different perspectives – catholic, protestant, jewish, black and second generation. We made contacts through a variety of routes – Irish organisations, *The Irish Post* newspaper, Irish women's conferences, word of mouth. Some women contacted us when they heard about the work we were doing. In all, we interviewed and photographed about eighty women and most of the interviewing was done in women's own homes. We planned to take two different kinds of photographs. Firstly, we wanted portraits of the women we interviewed and secondly, we wanted pictures which would present a view of Irish women within their community, in ways which would highlight their role and also capture the spirit of life of Irish people together. This process was started by photographing women at events such as St Patrick's night dance, Roundwood Festival and the Older Irish Women's Festival.

Initially, we envisaged the book as a series of portraits – whole life stories, but we altered this plan when it became clear that this would restrict the variety of experience. We decided, finally, on a combination of portraits and chapters concentrating on specific themes.

After background research, we built up a framework for the pictures and interviews. The questions we asked at the interviews were based on themes which can be grouped as follows:

(i) 'the common female realities'[3] – childbirth, sexuality, raising children;
(ii) common assumptions which exist about immigrant women – that they assimilate more easily than men; that women emigrate as the wives and daughters of male emigrants;
(iii) the influence of Irish background on women's lives – education, economic opportunities, political traditions, family, religion;
(iv) specific experiences of being Irish in England – arrival, work, opportunities, housing, cultural differences, racism.

So, a general outline of each women's life formed the basis of the interview, but with a slightly different emphasis each time. Sometimes, this emphasis was not the one which emerged most strongly during the interview, so we altered and revised our framework as we went along.

The interviews were lengthy, lasting a minimum of two hours and some women were interviewed more than once. Endless cups of tea, coffee, cakes and sometimes even whole meals were provided for us. The hospitality we encountered was extraordinary. The long interviews proved immensely useful because they allowed time for women to reflect on their experiences as well as describing and narrating them. Given that we had decided not to include our own commentary on what women told us, we were asking them to do this themselves. Also, extended interviews made it possible for subjects to come up which we hadn't foreseen. In general, a willingness to talk very openly about their lives was characteristic of the women we interviewed.

We had to rethink some of our original questions as we went along, in order to cover certain issues in more depth. Anti-Irish racism is an example of this. In the early interviews we found that women had quite differing perceptions of their experiences of hostility or prejudice. Direct questions such as, 'Have you ever experienced anti-Irish racism?' would sometimes draw a blank or simply a 'No'. Yet later on in the interview, the same woman would describe in detail how offensive she found certain comments about her accent or 'Irish jokes'. Certain kinds of questions would therefore have left important areas unexplored because of these differing perceptions and definitions. Where necessary then, we asked additional questions to try and get to grips with complex issues.

We also became aware of some implicit assumptions in our approach to the work as they grew more visible in the interviewing and editing process. An important example of this was the way that locating women in their social and political background was integral to our outlook. One woman we interviewed said, 'History is the beginning and the end of the Irish person,' and we certainly identified with this way of looking at it. A sense of our own history is very strong amongst Irish people in a way which people in Britain often find mystifying. Most women we talked to felt this. The need to locate ourselves historically also appears to be reinforced by living over here and confronting that lack of information which so many British people have about Ireland and also, about their own history. Against this background, many Irish people living in England feel that they can't afford not to know something about their own history.

Through the interviews we amassed a wealth of material, only some of which we've been able to use. The women whose lives, words and photographs appear in the book, obviously do not represent any definitive statement about Irish women's emigration, nor are they a random choice. In addition, the viewpoints expressed in the book don't necessarily reflect ours. We had dilemmas and arguments about what to include and how much to try and cover. There are many gaps; and there are other areas which we only manage to touch on and which need whole books in themselves. Our final choice of material was influenced by the restrictions we faced on time, word length, number of pictures possible and, of course, by our own perspective on the subject. Nevertheless, we feel convinced that the range of experience covered has a depth and a breadth which will evoke a wide response.

From Speech to Print

'Words the brisk herbs of language'[4]

A major issue we faced when editing the interviews, was how best to transfer the spoken word to the printed page. We wanted to convey the rhythms of Irish people's speech, the variety of phrases and expressions, the ways we use the English language and, in particular, the influence of the Irish language on this. Nevertheless, there is the constant fear that in writing the spoken word down, part of the meaning may be lost. Given the huge differences between the spoken and the written word, we sought some kind of bridge between the idioms of speech and tone of voice used, and the conventions of print. Our early editing was more adventurous in this respect but we found that we had to modify our approach as we progressed for a number of reasons. A practical difficulty we faced was that the women interviewed had a wide variety of Irish accents and some second generation women had English accents, so we couldn't work out a single system which would work consistently across the book. We needed a totally individual approach to each edit. As well as that, the initial transcribing of the interviews was crucial, we discovered, if the style of speaking was to be conveyed effectively.

The wider issue we faced was that of the relationship between language, power and status in this society, and in particular, the position which 'Standard English' – spoken and written – occupies in this. Working-class, regional and ethnic accents are not seen as equal parts of the whole and as simply different ways of speaking English. Instead, they are almost universally seen as inferior, incorrect or often, 'bad' English. At best, they may be viewed as quaint, colourful or unconventional.

This issue was really brought home to us when we were editing the book. The dilemma we faced was that, on the one hand, we wanted to convey the idiom of people's speech but we became increasingly aware that in general it is only working-class accents which are portrayed with phonetic spelling or distinct turns of phrases. Quite often, they are being either caricatured or trivialised in the process. Middle- and upper-class accents and speech are rarely written phonetically or presented as having their own set of eccentricities. Instead, they are presented as sounding exactly the same as Standard English which is obviously untrue. Exceptions to this type or portrayal are those writers who deliberately set out to capture and evoke the rhythms, richness and style of other kinds of English – Irish, Caribbean, African writers. This tradition is strong amongst Irish writers – Lady Gregory, Sean O'Casey, Patrick MacGill and more recently Frances Molloy, and their writing has underlined the limits of written Standard English and challenged its norms. But this kind of work has been primarily in the area of fiction.

For Irish people living here, accent is the main way in which they are identifiable, and often it is the focus of mockery. Many women, therefore, were uncomfortable at having their style of speaking portrayed very informally or colloquially, especially given the permanence attached to the printed word. Ultimately, the compromise we reached was to try to convey a sense of the speaker's style, rather than a more direct representation of her speech and idiom.

The Photography

'If I could tell the story in words, I wouldn't need to lug a camera'[5]

We faced some similar issues with the photography to those outlined above. Although only one of us was a photographer we tried to share editorial decisions as much as possible.

At a very early stage we decided to use groups of photographs together as photo essays to explore particular themes. One of these was women's work and in this instance it was clear to us that pictures can convey a variety and range which would be difficult to capture otherwise.

When taking the portrait photographs, women themselves were asked to become involved. We wanted them to present themselves to the camera in a setting that was discussed with them beforehand. Generally they wished to be portrayed quite formally rather than in a workaday or domestic setting. In all cases, the pictures add another dimension to their stories.

Documentary photography on the other hand is a solitary activity. It's impossible to chat all the time whilst working – it stops you being aware of the feelings and movements of people around you and stops you picking up

14

on their body language and gestures which are the stuff of pictures. So you drift around trying to be relaxed and alert. Sometimes you are fooled into thinking you have caught the atmosphere; you get drawn in, you can hear the sounds of the voices, the mood of participation and you imagine it must be in the pictures. But you get home and it isn't always there.

The editing of the pictures starts in the taking. Selections are made every time the shutter is pressed, decisions are immediate and final. A given moment does not repeat itself, so afterwards you are left with a series of images you can accept or reject depending on what you have decided to disclose of the situation photographed. That process consists of choosing a few frames from each film to be printed up for possible inclusion in the finished work. They too are subject to manipulations in the darkroom — aspects of a photograph can be highlighted or cropped. Editing therefore involves a technical, aesthetic and political interpretation. Through this long process you arrive at an overall view.

From the outset, we agreed with the women we interviewed and photographed that they would have the final say over how we used their material in the book. It seemed fundamental that we couldn't appropriate other people's lives without their consent. But as editors there was an inherent contradiction in this position. We obviously wanted to use the material which we felt worked best, which was strong, varied, but control over the material didn't ultimately lie with us, but with the contributors. We had the advantage of being familiar with all of the material and having, therefore, an overview, whereas individual women were only familiar with their part. In practice, we found that we were often in agreement, either total agreement or there were just minor differences. In some instances we disagreed significantly and a compromise was reached, and in one or two instances, the differences were irresolvable and we were unable to use the material. This process and the dilemmas which go with it for both the editors and contributors is built into the nature of a book like this one.

Reflections . . .

The experiences of women in the book speak for themselves. So many threads emerged from the interviews that we continually experienced a sense of discovery and excitement as well as a sense of frustration at not being able to follow some of them further. We want to comment on a few issues in particular.

Firstly, one common assumption about immigrant women is that they assimilate more easily than men, and we wanted to explore whether there was any truth in this. We set out to discuss adaptation to British society and what began to emerge was a complex picture. None of the women who emigrated from Ireland considered herself to have 'assimilated' – to have become absorbed into this society. They all identified themselves very much as Irish.

15

(This issue is obviously different for the second generation women.)

Many women felt that England was now their home, but nevertheless this did not diminish their sense of being Irish. Without doubt though, what became clear was that women face greater pressures to adapt to British society than men, because of their family role and responsibilities. They are the ones who have to deal with British institutions – they go to the health centres, schools, hospitals, playgrounds and when necessary negotiate these situations. These are also the situations where attitudes to the Irish, reactions to Irish accents are unavoidable and can have a real bearing on the treatment you receive. The firmly established tradition of Irish men leaving these areas of responsibility to women reinforces their role and the pressures they often face. The family orientation of the Irish community influences its social and welfare networks and because of this, single women may not have very strong links with it. This can be isolating since the community does in its own way provide a safety net for its members. The interviews bear out that the cost of adapting to living in a different society is sometimes very great or simply ongoing hard work. The high incidence of mental illness amongst Irish women in Britain may be, in part, a reflection of this.

Obviously what emerged from our interviews is not a comprehensive look at this subject. Because of the nature of our book and our network of contacts we talked primarily to women who have links, in one way or another, with the Irish community, rather than those who might consider themselves to have assimilated. But it has certainly led us to question what 'assimilate' actually means and the many different ways it might be defined.

We asked all of the women we interviewed to comment on areas of female sexuality such as childbirth, learning about sex, sexual relationships with other women. These are obviously massively important for all women but nevertheless very often shrouded in silence. On top of that, the links between sexuality and childbirth, for example, are usually ignored or denied. Several different strands emerged from this. Many women commented on the way that ideas about sexuality were communicated to them as a child and that difficulties were created for them when these were communicated in the negative or fearful way. However, alongside that, a sense of fatalism about childbirth and its pain was accepted by some women and we encountered mixed feelings amongst the women we talked to about the value or usefulness of exploding the conspiracy of silence surrounding it. Some felt it was vital to be told more about it beforehand in order to better prepare yourself, whilst others felt it was not an experience you could be prepared for. Another strand was the ways in which the anonymity of living in another country and culture can allow more possibilities for women in areas of sexuality – coming out as a lesbian and the possibility of getting a divorce and marrying again were two striking examples of this.

We were not always able to follow through discussions on female sexuality. We found that women, including ourselves, do not always find it easy to talk about 'common female realities'. This is not really surprising given the taboos surrounding many of them and the way in which aspects of female sexuality are pushed into the 'private' domain and so remain untold history among women generally – 'Telling the truth about one's experience as a body, forbidden, not possible for centuries.'[6]

Another important thread was the way in which Irish political traditions are viewed in this country. The failure to recognise that Irish people bring with them their own distinct traditions can create conflicts. Women described how republicanism is not accepted as a valid political position. Instead it is assumed that it is an emotional reaction. Equally, it's often assumed that all Irish women come from rural backgrounds and therefore, don't know about trade unions. The same kinds of assumptions are often applied to feminism – that Irish women have to come to England to learn about it. These conflicts extend into the second generation where women are confronted by two clashing versions of history at home and at school. Examples of British 'heroism' or 'radicalism' are very often precisely the events which to an Irish person represent British oppression and violence. The role of Cromwell in Britain and in Ireland is one dramatic example of this.

Finally, we asked all of the women interviewed to comment on the role that religion had played or continued to play in their lives. For many, the experience of being catholic in England is totally different from their experience in Ireland. It means being a member of a minority religion as opposed to a majority religion, but also of an unpopular religion. Even though we start from a critical perspective on the Catholic Church, we have found the strand of anti-catholicism virulent in England – that 'inherited dormant violence of anti-Popery'[7] – very disconcerting and irrational.

In common with other immigrant communities, religion is important for Irish people as a point of contact with home, and as a source of community feeling on arrival. It offers a familiar point on an otherwise strange landscape. It is also a way of marking your difference and separateness from the host community. The Catholic Church has provided social and welfare services for the Irish community which has reinforced the link between Irishness and catholicism for many. It does seem to us though, that for more recent arrivals, this is changing. From the interviews, it seems that many women do adhere to their religion but often feel an ambivalence about its moral positions. Living in large cities, they encounter a more secular environment and more opportunities to make choices about moral issues. They often appear to modify their attitudes and avail of contraception, divorce, abortion, even if this conflicts with their religion. Other women, for whom religion has ceased to be relevant while living in Ireland, continued to have no contact with it here and often rejected it because it represented institutionalised misogyny. Yet others found themselves in a position where having ceased to practise catholicism, they still wanted contact with networks it offered, particularly when it came to sending their children to school.

17

The Last Word ...

We want this book to contribute to the Irish community's sense of itself and draw attention to the role that women play in it. Unless women's contribution and perspective are fully known and recognised, the overall picture is distorted and inadequate and part of our history is lost to us. Given the alarming rate at which Irish emigration is increasing at the present time, this sense of our history seems even more crucial to know and hold on to. We also hope the book will challenge some of the notions which exist outside our community about the Irish, and Irish women in particular. Last, but not least, we hope you enjoy reading it.

Notes

1. See Liz Curtis, *Ireland the Propoganda War: the British media and the 'battle for hearts and minds'*, Pluto Press, London, 1986.
2. Over 6,000 people have been detailed under PTA. Less than two per cent have been charged with offences under the Act.
3. Tillie Olsen, *Silences*, p. 43, Virago Press, London, 1980.
4. Eavan Boland, 'The Oral Tradition', in *The Journey and other poems*, p.14, Carcanet & Arlen House, Manchester & Dublin, 1986.
5. Lewis Hine in Susan Sontag, *On Photography*, p. 185, Penguin, London, 1979.
6. Tillie Olsen, *Silences*, p. 254.
7. Elizabeth Bowen's introduction to Antonia White, *Frost in May*, p. x, Virago Press, London, 1977.

Historical Background

Our version of the world

In this chapter we will look at some of the events which we feel are relevant background to Irish women's emigration. To start with, we would like to outline the broader context in which we are considering these events – the domination of our country by British colonialism and the inferior status of women in society. As a people, our history is distorted and buried by centuries of British rule. As women we feel the weight of this oppression on behalf of our foremothers, but also on behalf of all our people. We feel integrated in our country's history in a way which is common among colonised peoples, but which is often seen as strange, or is misunderstood, by British women. We recognise that as women this makes our own history twice-buried. In common with women from societies around the world, our past is hidden from us and we are reduced to sifting through what is recorded by powerful and vested male interests for clues about the lives, interests and conditions of our sex. In Irish history powerful women do exist, and their stories are sometimes well-documented, but we know very little about the lives 'ordinary' women led.

Before the 1600s Ireland was still mainly a tribal society and the position of women was very different from that of women in the feudal states which existed in the rest of Europe at that time. Although a patriarchy, Gaelic Ireland operated under the Brehon Laws,[1] which gave women unusual status – in many respects equal to that of men of the same social rank. However, the sixteenth century saw the beginning of the destruction of this society by a series of campaigns, notably during the Elizabethan and Cromwellian eras, which aimed to colonise the whole of Ireland more efficiently for English benefit. A policy of plantation was embarked on, in Ulster in 1609 and after Cromwell's atrocities in 1653, to name just two examples. The Irish were forced off their lands. Many were banished, by a specific date, to the poorest land on the western seaboard where room was found for them by confiscating the land of those already there. Others were sold to the West Indies as indentured labour, including women and children. By the end of the Cromwellian era, some 85 per cent of the land had been expropriated by English colonists at one time or another.

A century of unprecedented ferocity against the Irish culminated in a final onslaught on distinctive Irish ways of life when, in 1692, the Penal Laws were introduced against catholics and dissenters. The Irish language, customs and other expressions of culture were outlawed and severely penalised. An education system through the medium of English was imposed. The bulk of Irish people were discriminated against in all aspects of society, and as a result of these measures, they gradually became distinguishable from the ruling classes by their poverty and alienation. As far as our interests as women were concerned, 'in its attitude to women and their place in society ... modern Ireland enjoys no continuity with its Gaelic past'.[2]

English domination had an enormous impact on the development of Irish society, and every aspect came under attack. Throughout the next two centuries the country began to develop along lines dictated by English economic necessity. Trade and industry were systematically suppressed where they came into conflict with these interests and exploited in the cases where they didn't. The Irish woollen and linen industries are good examples – the first flourishing trade being totally destroyed as England tried to build her own, the latter being encouraged in the north-east of Ireland as there was no English competitor. The Irish glass industry was also destroyed.

In the mid-1800s four-fifths of the Irish population lived on the land, in most cases the poorest land available where their ancestors had been banished during the Cromwellian era. The land system was exploitative and confined the majority of people to very small farms with high rents – paid for in grain and other foodstuffs. The people were marginalised in their own country and by the time of the potato failures of 1845, 1846 and 1847, such was the condition of the ordinary Irish person that half a million were lost to their country during the Great Hunger, either through death by starvation or disease, or through emigration. The failure of the potato crop was general throughout Europe, only in Ireland did it result in famine – the culmination of colonial policies and their disastrous consequences.

In addition, English policies with regard to land and trade in Ireland created both immediate and long-term factors leading to the growth of emigration. Over the previous two centuries growing numbers left Ireland. Seasonal harvesters travelled back and forth, including many women and children. The eighteenth-century agricultural revolution in England drew many Irish labourers. By 1841, just before the Famine, there were some 400,000 Irish people living in Britain.

The Famine brought to catastrophic proportions a pattern of emigration which had already been set. It was nonetheless a turning point, and has left an indelible mark. Mass emigration, and the pattern of women leaving – of the kind that makes the stories in this book familiar to every Irish family – began then. Within twenty years the population of Ireland was reduced by two million.

The scale of emigration from Ireland after 1850 is so enormous that it is unequalled anywhere else in Europe. Against this general picture is the pattern of Irish women's emigration, which developed some unusual features over the next period. The bulk of emigration was to America rather than to Britain, and in the mid-1800s Irish women made up 35 per cent of Irish immigrants there. From this time onwards they left primarily as single women, and generally, they left at a younger age than men. Also, as the century progressed and during many periods of the twentieth century, more women than men emigrated. This is untypical amongst emigrant groups. Women began to predominate amongst Irish emigrants to the United States in the 1880s and in the 1890s amongst those to Britain. In the United States, where figures do exist, this predominance of women is in striking contrast to other immigrant groups – Irish women making up 52.9 per cent of all Irish immigrants, whereas the comparable figure for Southern Italy was 21 per cent and for Germany, 41 per cent.

So why was the pattern of Irish women's emigration different? Changes in Irish society after the famine are relevant. Sub-division of land was

Emigrants on the quay, c 1840.

widespread prior to the famine, but post-famine agitation led to a number of Land Acts giving tenants more rights, gradually introducing the right to buy, finalised as late as 1903. A system of inheritance by one family member, in order to consolidate small farms as economically viable units, gradually replaced the old sub-division of farms. It was normally a son who inherited. This, of course, meant that women had little chance of inheriting or sharing the family farm, and prospects of marrying into one were also reduced. The policy of deliberate underdevelopment of Irish industry and trade meant that the towns and cities were small and the possibilities of employment limited, so many young, single women had little option but to emigrate.

The development of the dowry system across all classes may also have contributed to women's emigration. Dowries had been common among better-off farmers and landed gentry, but with the changes in land inheritance it became more widespread. A woman bringing a dowry of money, cattle or land was a better match than a woman with nothing. This often meant that arranged marriages overtook love matches. For many families providing a dowry for all their daughters was impossible, but emigration could have provided an opportunity for a woman to earn her own, or possibly to contribute to a younger sister's.

Irish women who emigrated played a very important economic role in relation to their families, their communities back home, and the countries to which they emigrated. Having left Ireland to find work, thereby contributing to the host community, they supported themselves, sent financial help home, and often assisted other members of the family with their passage.

In the fifty years after the famine Irish women arriving in England seem to have settled mainly in the large cities, although some did take up agricultural labouring. Industrialisation in Lancashire and Western Scotland absorbed many women into the factories and mills producing linen, wool and hosiery. In London, Irish women went into domestic service in large numbers. It provided them with their accommodation, which was a crucial consideration for women alone and it required no previous training to start, other than a willingness to work long, hard hours. In 1851, 42.7 per cent of Irish women in London were servants, whilst the second largest occupation was clothing. The pattern was similar in the east coast cities of America, where the name 'Bridget' became synonymous with 'domestic servant'.[3] There they monopolised this area of work, and were unique amongst immigrant groups in taking it up in large numbers. One contributory factor to this may be that by this time most Irish women would have been able to speak some English, giving them greater accessibility to this work than other European immigrant women would have had initially.

Research into conditions for Irish immigrants in the English Victorian cities confirms that 'the great majority entered the lowliest and least healthy urban occupations'.[4] They were outsiders, coming to the home of the traditional enemy. They grouped together in Irish ghettoes in Liverpool,

York, Glasgow and other cities. The majority were catholic, and catholicism – a symbol of resistance in Irish history – was often a badge of separate identity in Britain. The Church, and catholic schools in particular, represented some measure of familiarity. For their part the native communities often greeted the Irish with antagonism and racism, and anti-catholic feeling was often directed against Irish communities.

Emigration begets emigration ... by the end of the nineteenth century the pattern was firmly set. More women were leaving than men, and sisters, aunts, cousins and friends abroad became an encouragement to those at home to follow.

Back in Ireland, the twentieth century opened with renewed efforts by the people to rid themselves of British domination. The war of independence, the bitter and traumatic events of the 1916 Rising and of the Civil War years, and the final *de facto* recognition of partition shaped an Ireland which many believed was neither free nor independent in any real sense. In the decade after 1922 – when partial independence had been achieved – several administrations were elected. However, in common with the experiences since of other colonies after independence, much of the British legal and bureaucratic structures, including the civil service, remained intact. The legacy of emigration too lived on, and was to rise to alarming new levels.

The policies pursued by Irish governments over the next fifty years not only failed to recognise the work women had done in achieving even partial independence, but in many cases actively legislated against women's rights in crucial areas, especially reproduction and employment. Women had been organised and indispensible fighters in the nationalist movement and the struggle for independence, for example, in the Ladies' Land League, Inghinidhe na hEireann, Cumann na mBan, and the Citizen's Army. In addition, many republican women and others outside this movement struggled on their own behalf, putting forward demands for votes and other rights for women; for instance, organising the Irishwomen's Franchise League, and the Irish Women Workers' Union. They were now to witness their horizons being gradually narrowed, both socially and economically, and particularly with the election in 1932 of the Fianna Fáil party[6] to government.

In 1935, contraceptives were banned with the passing of the Criminal Amendment Act, a situation which has remained virtually unchanged since, although they are now legally available to 'married couples'. In 1936 the Conditions of Employment Act was passed. This had major implications for women's position in the labour force. There were fixed ratios of women in certain jobs. Married women were barred from working in the state sector, and, as most of the private sector followed suit, were effectively banned from working in all but the most lowly-paid and traditional women's jobs. Feminists and women trade unionists actively opposed these measures, but they had general support. Women in rural Ireland also faced limited options. The Land Commission, set up in 1882, was charged after independence with redistributing large estates[7] to make small farms more viable. Although specifically acknowledging that women's role was crucial to the running of a successful farm, they nevertheless decided that women alone could not be considered for additions of land, and that families with sons took priority over those with only daughters. Many women had little option in these circumstances but to emigrate in search of work.

The pressures on women to emigrate were further increased by the proposed new Constitution, and by the way women's role was defined in it. This Constitution was voted for by barely one-third of the electorate in 1937 and, slightly amended, remains the Constitution of Ireland to this day. Article 41 states that 'by her life within the home, woman gives to the state a support without which the common good cannot be achieved'. At the time, many women opposed this, but an amendment put by a woman in the parliamentary debate on the Constitution, to recognise that all women contributed to the common good, whether working inside or outside the home, was defeated. The Constitution went further, and declared 'that mothers shall not be obliged by economic necessity to engage in labour to the neglect of their duties in the home'. The effect of these clauses was to define women as mothers, and the pious implication that they would receive recognition and support for this work was never fulfilled. Having effectively denied them access to paid work, provision for women in terms of pensions, child benefit, health care and so on was woefully inadequate, or even non-existent, as in the case of single parents.

The special position of the Catholic Church in Irish society was also enshrined in the Constitution. The result of this was that on social and sexual issues in particular, its views were often imposed in the form of legislation which bound even those of other religious persuasions, or of none. It also created a social climate antagonistic to women's needs, as the illegality of contraception and divorce, for example, shows. The consequence of these kinds of attitudes and policies was a high level of emigration of young single women which grew steadily.

The advent of World War II had an important effect on emigration from Ireland. During the war Britain needed to supplement its labour force and it automatically turned to its traditional source, Ireland. This dramatically underlined the extent to which the economic relationship between the two countries remained unchanged by political independence. The Irish State was officially neutral – in practice it was 'neutral on England's side'. Thousands of Irish men and women, from north and south of the border, joined the British Army. Many more left for Britain, directly recruited by the British authorities to fill the gaps in the labour force. Recruitment posters appeared in the labour exchanges in Ireland urging women to join the forces, apply for jobs and come and help in the war effort. Emigrants often arrived in England with the names of their employers pinned to their lapels. Given its own economic problems, the Fianna Fáil government turned an official blind eye, and went

24

along with the option of exporting its surplus labour. Many women found that the war presented them with opportunities they would have been denied in more normal times. By the end of the war, the numbers of Irish women in Britain in nursing, factory work and clerical work were rising, and the numbers in domestic work were falling.

In the aftermath of the war Britain was rebuilding its economy and its need for workers was greater than ever. Irish people left for Britain in their hundreds of thousands, and it was during this wave of emigration, a particularly great haemorrhage of people from the land, that the numbers of women over men emigrating reached its highest point. The Commission on Emigration, reporting in 1956, stated 'The male-female ratio in the 26 Counties is exceptional by comparison with European countries, where, in general, the female population exceeds the male.' In Ireland, males have been in the majority at each census since 1911. It is astonishing that this female exodus, on a scale which affected the social and economic development of the whole country, seems to have been ignored by successive governments and opposition parties. Whole communities withered, their roots torn away, whole villages became totally deserted, and rural Ireland in particular went into a dramatic decline. As the social and economic opportunities diminished even further for those left behind, another cycle of emigration was ensured.

An independent Ireland held a promise which, for women especially, had been completely dashed. Their inferior status and lack of opportunity at home could not be weighed against the pull of an expanding economy in Britain. Many women did not find it easy to leave, as they explain in the following pages. Nor did they turn their backs on Ireland – for many it was a way of investing in the community they came from. In the 1950s, net remittances from emigrants made up £12m of Ireland's gross national product. The contribution towards this figure from Irish women abroad will have been significant.

It was at this time, during the war and after, that significant differences emerged between emigration from both sides of the border, and the level in the North fell in contrast with that in the South. The economy in the North received a boost during the war years and work was more plentiful. After the war, the Six Counties benefitted from the expansion of the British economy as a whole, the introduction of the National Health Service, the expansion of education, and the public housing programmes which were a feature of the 1950s. The nationalist population, trapped behind the border, were systematically discriminated against, notably in housing[8] and employment, and rapidly became identifiable in terms of relative disadvantage and poverty, as well as through their politics.

The Irish who settled in Britain during this time had much in common with those who went before. They settled together in the cities they arrived in and expanded their community by taking in relatives as they arrived in turn. Almost everybody had family here, and it was often the women in the family to whom the new emigrants came, and who did the work of supporting and initiating them in their first weeks here. A main point of contact for emigrants in those days was the Catholic Church. After Sunday Mass unofficial advice and information was exchanged, and officially, the Church organised schools, welfare work, references for jobs, even recreation, as Irish centres and sports clubs were often attached to the local church or catholic school. The Counties Associations were also active in all these fields. Emigrants from each country in Ireland belonged to their own association and organised music and dancing for children, recreation for adults and especially fund-raising activities to help those in need. Irish women organised and ran much of this welfare work, and they were also in the forefront in keeping alive Irish ways and culture, for instance organising children's participation in Feiseanna.[9]

Although the profile of the community was low during these years, they nevertheless suffered hostility from outside. Notices such as 'No Irish need apply' and 'No Irish, No Coloureds', were common in the 1950s and '60s, especially when looking for accommodation. Alongside this, however, many Irish women benefitted from what appear to be contradictions in Britain's use of women immigrants' labour. Irish women were able to take up opportunities not as easily available to black women at this time – for example SRN training, with its higher status and better promotion prospects, rather than SEN, in nursing. In addition, Irish women had, at times, better access to white collar work such as banking, teaching and so on, than had Irish men. The employment opportunities for immigrant groups in Britain is obviously part of a complex picture which changes over time, and can be subject to dramatic reversals, as many 1980s Irish emigrants are now experiencing.

During the economic boom of the 1960s and the 1970s, emigration from Ireland began to fall for the first time. Foreign multinationals were induced by huge tax-free incentives to set up plants in Ireland, often in rural areas. This resulted in a period of economic prosperity during which many Irish emigrants returned home. Membership of the European Economic community also served to dilute Britain's economic influence. It is interesting to note, that in spite of this relative prosperity, more men than women returned to Ireland. Things had not changed significantly for women since the 1930s. In the late 1960s and '70s, however, in common with women in many other countries, Irish women began to organise around their own interests, and to fight their oppression. The battles women fought in Ireland were both specific to their own situation and universal – child benefits payable to mothers, benefits for single parents, access to contraception and abortion, the right to divorce, the right to self-defined sexuality, equal employment opportunities and equal pay. Some of these battles have been won. In particular, Irish women won the right to equal pay for work of equal value, still being argued for by British women who only have the right to equal pay for the same work. But the struggle continues.

26

This period of relative prosperity and net immigration into Ireland was, however, shortlived. The multinationals were putting little, if any of the profits they made back into the Irish economy. Between 1980 and 1985, £4.034m in profits was taken out of Ireland by the big multinationals. Against this background there have been some enormous setbacks in relation to women's rights. In spite of the removal of the section of the Constitution recognising the special position of the Catholic Church, in 1983 an amendment was passed by referendum of the people which enshrines the right to life of a foetus as equal to that of the mother. Abortion was already illegal in Ireland, now it is illegal to provide women with information about its availability elsewhere. In 1986 a proposal to allow divorce was also defeated.

Against this background, and that of world economic recession, Irish emigration began to rise dramatically and is now being compared with some of the highest peaks in the past. In May 1987, Fr Frank Ryan, director of a hostel in Kilburn, said 'I would compare the current levels not with those of the 1940s or '50s, but with famine times.' The most recent figures also suggest an increase in the number of graduates leaving. In 1986 only 64 per cent of graduates found employment in Ireland, and some British local authorities are now sending teams to Ireland to recruit teachers for vacant jobs here. The Irish taxpayer is subsidising the British economy very directly in these instances.

The Irish government has adopted very contradictory poses on the issue, pledging help on the one hand, and on the other, emphasising the individual's

London picket (1985) in support of Joanne Hayes accused of murdering her newborn baby

right to leave. The solution proposed by one politician was that the Irish should use their 'legal right of access to Europe' and parents ensure that their children learn foreign languages.

Irish people arriving in Britain today also face a very different situation. At many points in the past the British, although antagonistic and hostile, needed a large number of Irish workers. The employment situation has changed markedly today and anti-Irish racism is vociferous and harassment and discrimination common. Two very clear examples of the kind of treatment Irish people may expect have recently come to light. In June 1987, the DHSS in many London boroughs began to systematically treat Irish people with suspicion and, for example, their copy birth certificates from Ireland were unacceptable as proof of identity. Later in the same year it came to light that Camden housing department was offering to pay fares back to Ireland for Irish families who qualified for housing, irrespective of the length of time they had lived in Britain.

The ways in which the Irish community, and Irish women in particular, organise to oppose this racism and harassment will be crucial. Irish women's work and struggle in supporting each other as immigrant women in an often hostile environment has a long established history, though much of this has obviously happened on an informal basis. In recent years, new ways of organising have developed. The London Irish Women's Centre opened in 1986, and many Irish women's groups meet regularly, engaging in both activities and discussion around issues as varied as culture, politics and welfare. There are Irish language mother and toddler groups, an Irish Women's Abortion Support Group, prisoners' support work, women's bands, to name only a few. These networks will be important to women coming in this new wave of emigration. Alongside all this, however, we should not forget that the present level of emigration means that even larger numbers of women join past generations lost to Ireland.

Notes

1. The Brehon Laws, dating from as early as the seventh century, consist of the customs of Irish society, as refined and elaborated by a specialist class of legal scholars of the time. They contain a great deal of information on the status of women.
2. D. O Corráin, 'Women in Early Irish Society' in *Women in Irish Society*, M. MacCurtain and D. O Corráin, eds., p. 11, Arlen House, Dublin, 1978.
3. See Hasia R. Diner, *Erin's Daughters in America – Irish Immigrant Women in the Nineteenth Century*, John Hopkins University Press, Baltimore, 1983.
4. Sheridan Gilley, 'The Irish' in *History Today*, vol 35, June 1985.
5. An uprising against British rule in 1916 – also called the Easter Rising. Headquarters were in the General Post Office in Dublin. Seven leaders were subsequently executed.

6. De Valera resigned from Sinn Féin after the defeat of his proposal that those elected should take up their seats in the Dáil (parliament) if the oath of allegiance to the British monarch was abolished. Two months later, in May 1926, he founded a new party, Fianna Fáil. In the general election of 1932 it secured an overall majority and formed the government. It has retained power in the great majority of elections in the State since that time.
7. The estates of absentee English landlords, and those who left Ireland after independence, were subject to compulsory purchase by the State and redistributed among small farmers to make viable farms.
8. In order to have a local authority vote, you had to be a householder, and therefore any discrimination against catholics in terms of housing had political repercussions.
9. Events where the best practitioners of various Irish traditional arts – singing, dancing, music – are judged and awarded prizes for excellence.

Arrivals

The tradition of emigration from Ireland is reflected in our culture. The experience has touched every Irish family's life. Irish women grow up knowing they have relatives in many distant places; Irish people have emigrated to every part of the world. Evidence of this is not just in the songs, stories and poetry of Ireland but all around them. At certain periods, whole villages have been deserted, and often communities have recreated themselves in other parts of the world as people gradually leave to join those who have already gone, to places they already feel connected to through a long line of emigrants. This continues to be true at the present time. The closeness of Britain also makes emigration easier. It allows for the illusion that it is possible to come and stay for a short while, and eventually return home.

The pattern was set

'I REMEMBER my sisters going to America in the 1920s and crying and all this business. And I remember the money coming . . . once two of them went, the money soon came for the third one when they were old enough to go, and this is how it went on. And you must remember, in those days they never came back. Nobody ever saw their face again.'

*

'EMIGRATION altered the landscape. My uncle who was born in 1896 used to say he remembered eighty families living on our country road, during his childhood. He could name them and point out their houses. But when we were growing up there in the 1950s, there weren't more than a dozen families.'

An abandoned farmhouse in Maam Valley, Co. Galway

Exodus of 20,250 Girls from the West of Ireland.

List of Subscriptions received from 1880 to 1884, Report, and List of nearly 1,200 Clergymen, with the number of persons applied for by each.

LIST OF SUBSCRIPTIONS RECEIVED,

More than Nine-tenths of them being entirely unsolicited.

	£	s	d
The Duchess of Marlborough (from the balance of her Irish Relief Fund)	£100	0	0
Right Hon. W. E. Forster, M.P. (when Chief Secretary for Ireland)	100	0	0
James H. Tuke, Hitchin, Herts	100	0	0
Committee of Mr. Tuke's Emigration Fund	130	0	0
Charles Wilson, Cheltenham (two sums of £100 each)	200	0	0
Joshua Dixon, Tarporley, Cheshire (three sums of £100 each)	300	0	0
S. S. E., London (three sums of £100 each)	300	0	0
S. A. S., London (four sums of £100 each)	400	0	0
W. Rathbone, M.P.	100	0	0

Collected by S. Laing, M.P.—

	£	s	d
C. Waring, Esq.	£25	0	0
Mrs. Byass	5	0	0
Theresa Byass	4	0	0
Lady Georgiana Pakenham	2	0	0
T. Walker, Esq.	2	2	0
E. Kennard, Esq.	5	0	0
Mrs. Kennard	1	0	0
C. Macrae, Esq.	4	0	0
Mrs. Macrae	1	0	0
H. Laing, Esq.	2	10	0
Members of the London Stock Exchange, per H. Laing	8	0	0
S. Laing, M.P. (in two sums of £50 each)	100	0	0
Mrs. Laing	10	0	0
Sundry other Subscriptions	25	0	0
	194	12	0

	£	s	d
Blackie & Son, Glasgow	35	0	
Right Hon. G. Cubitt, M.P.	25	0	
Bolton King, Green Street, London	25	0	
Samuel J. M'Caughey, Coonong, New South Wales	25	0	
The Most Rev. Dr. ——, R. C. Bishop of —— (in two sums of £10 each)	20	0	
The Duke of Devonshire	20	0	
S. S.	20	0	

	£	s	d
John Ward, Belfast	£20	0	0
Rev. E. Redmond, D.D., Chudleigh, Devon	15	0	0
The Earl of Morny	10	0	0
Hon. A. K. Digby, London	10	0	0
Earl Clermont	10	0	0
Lady Vere Cameron (in two sums of £5 each)	10	0	0
R. N. Philips, M.P.	10	0	0
Rev. J. C. Street, Belfast	6	0	0
The Marchioness (Louisa) of Waterford	5	0	0
The Earl of Shaftesbury	5	0	0
The Earl of Derby	5	0	0
The Earl of Carysfort	5	0	0
Lord O'Hagan	5	0	0
William Ewart, M.P.	5	0	0
F. C. Capel	5	0	0
John Rboney, Ballina	5	0	0
Miss Margaret A. Hardwick, Burgess Hill, Sussex	3	10	0
R. B. Heathcote, Friday Hill	2	4	0
Mrs. R. B. Heathcote, Friday Hill	2	4	0
Miss Mabel S. Crawford, Cannes	2	2	0
C. T. Redington, H. M. Commissioner of Emigration	2	2	0
—t O'Brien, Ballybrack	2	2	0
	2	0	0
	0	0	0

'MY FATHER like most fathers in the area went to England for seasonal work. I mean, he'd been going there since he was fifteen. We took it totally for granted. This was no exception, it was the rule in the families around. I remember I hardly knew him until I was six or seven, so when he came back it was like a stranger in the house but he was still our father and we were very aware of that. We were obviously still close to him and he was extremely good. He always wrote for our birthdays and he came back every summer and at Christmas.'

There was work across the water

'I STOPPED school in 1929 when I was fourteen. There was no jobs then or the pay was nothing, if you managed to get one. I went out working on the farm with my father and brother. We worked very hard – we all had to do our bit. After four years on the farm, I left and came over here.'

*

'THERE were no opportunities for women in Ireland in my day. If a woman got married and then started to work in the 1930s, she'd be criticised all over the place. "God, she didn't make much of a match, he can't even keep her." It never dawned on anybody that a person might like to go out to work. But that meant there was never an opening for a woman. You couldn't take up a decent job, because you'd be expected to leave the minute you got married.'

*

'NOW my sisters came home from England and said, "You should come back with us," although I was still earning a good bit at home teaching Irish dancing in the town hall. I didn't have to come away at that time, but my sisters said, "You must come to England. What are you doing here? There'll be nothing here for you. You must come." And I came.'

*

'AS FAR as job options went in the sixties, there was only the Civil Service or the local county council. That was it. If you could get into either of those, you were made. University wasn't even discussed except for the most brilliant – so that wasn't an option at all. I'd love to have gone to university but my parents could never have afforded to subsidise me while I studied in Dublin.'

*

'I LEFT school in 1956. But it was hard as a catholic to find work, because when I went for an interview the first question that they asked was what church you went to. Another girl that went to school with me, and her marks weren't anything like mine, applied for the same job as me. She was a protestant and she got it.'

Working in the bog:
Gathering turf in for the winter, 1890s and 1985

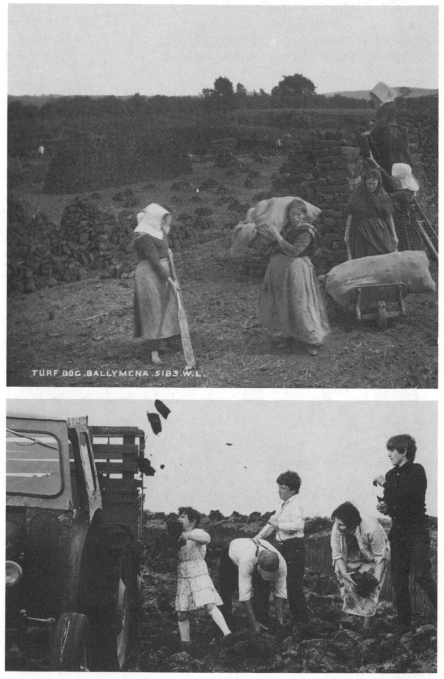

Sunday Press advertisement for nurses, 1987
Inset: London transport recruitment poster for women conductors,
1942

STAFF NURSES

Come and see
what awaits you in London

The Promise
Unique

You'll be working in one of two National Hospitals in the middle of London's West End, which have been recognised as being the birthplace of Neurology.

And apart from living and working in the heart of one of the world's most exciting cities, there's the professional challenge of getting involved in Neurology where major breakthroughs in both treatment and diagnosis are being made all the time.

We promise a minimum salary of £7,500 + allowance.

And to get on your feet we'll pay your UKCC registration fees: your air fare from Ireland: provide you with FREE accommodation for the first month: and GUARANTEED accommodation thereafter.

The Prospects
Unlimited

A ....enced Staff Nurses we are looking f............................run the most.

The Places

THE NATIONAL HOSPITALS QUEEN SQUARE & MAIDA VALE

The National Hospi

Enjoy your War Work

Can't look in the blackout

GOOD PAY · FREE UNIFORM AND AN INTERESTING JOB

LONDON NEEDS MORE WOMEN
BUS AND TRAM CONDUCTORS

SEE LARGE POSTERS FOR PARTICULARS

Leavetaking

'I DECIDED anyway that I'd go. So I said one week to my mother that I was going to England. She said, "You're not." They had an awful dislike against you coming to England. So I said, "I am." "Well," she said, "I wish I was burying you instead of letting you go to England." But I came anyway. I made up my own mind.'

*

'I DON'T think I would have left as easily if I hadn't known somebody who was living over here. My friend Barbara was in the Midlands. But I mean a lot of people emigrated on their own, especially to England. They just came, some without money or friends or anything. I couldn't have done that.'

*

Family gathering in Dublin, 1943

Ticket office, Dun Laoghaire harbour

'So, my sister, her boyfriend and me sat by the fire talking one night and all of a sudden the three of us decided, just like that, to come over here and see if we could find work. And it was a great big adventure to come over, but we were actually frightened as well.'

*

'My mother didn't really raise any objections. I think she knew I could take care of myself, basically. But my father was horrified, heartbroken. He had sisters here in England and all his life he had been going down to Rosslare to meet them off the boat, usually in the small hours of the morning with small children. He was very close to his sisters, and now it was starting all over again with me. We never really communicated in words, but we were close. We knew we loved each other and that's all that mattered. He never believed I'd come back to live. You know, I did. I assumed I might come back. But my father knew the pattern was set and it was highly unlikely that I'd come back.'

The echoing footsteps

'IN THE MAY of 1939, I came by boat. Cried all the way. On the train and everything, cried and cried and more cried.'

Opposite: No seats on the night sailing
Below: Returning from a holiday in Ireland

Opposite: Asleep on a crowded boat-train
Above: A bit of crack on the way

'WHEN the train stopped at Euston, we sat in the train and – this shows you how green we were – the porter came round and said, "Everybody off." And we said, "Oh, we're going to London." He said, "You are in London!" So off we got.'

*

'I FLED to England with as many children as I could manage. I was heading for Reading because there were factories in Slough that I thought I could get work at and get a flat and provide for the kids.'

The first glimpse

'MY FIRST impression when I arrived in the early sixties was astonishment that I couldn't understand the language. I couldn't make head nor tail of the accents. That was a major problem for me, to understand what they were saying and the speed at which they spoke. And the other thing was the notice boards – "No Blacks, No Irish, and No Dogs." That astonished me. That was everywhere. When I'd hear an Irish accent, I used to say, "Hello," but they didn't really want to know me.'

*

41

'So, I landed on Kingston Station, and I wished I was behind in Kenmare. I was sick and fed up. There was a man on the platform who saw me there. He was there because they used to draw all the foodstuffs from the train by horse and cart – there was no such thing as lorries then. I asked him if there was a café around because it was seven o'clock in the morning. "Have you been travelling all night?" he asked. "Yes," I said. "Have you a job?" I said, "No, I haven't." "Well," he said, "I was delivering yesterday out in Thames Ditton and there was a woman there who asked me if I could find her a maid. So if you like, I'll take you out there." 'Course I was as innocent – I said, "OK, grand, yes great." So, I waited in the café and he came back and took me out there. I saw the woman, I don't know what she said to me but she employed me there and then.

At that time – it was the early thirties – in this country, they were really anxious for the Irish girls because they were strong and they'd do the work. She gave me an apron to put on and start work. There was no "Go to bed and rest!" She knew I'd been travelling all night. They didn't care. I put the apron on and I started. They were going out so she said, "We'll have so-and-so for dinner and rice pudding." I never said a word, but that was the first time I'd ever seen rice in my life! And you know, I managed.'

*

Waterloo station, London

On the tube, London

'I DIDN'T know what to think of London. There were crowds everywhere and I didn't know where all the people were coming from or going to. I'd come now from a rural area where you saw the lads once a week, unless they were going to the well or something. And now I'd come over here and everybody was knocking you down. I was bewildered. I remember well the underground, going on the tube and then the moving stairs. I was awful afraid until I got used to it.'

*

'IT WAS a relief to get away, such a relief. There was no fear in my life anymore. I wasn't waiting for somebody violent to come home. And I had my own money, I wasn't dependent.'

*

'IT'S VERY odd looking back on it now, but I'd no conception of England before I came. I didn't question coming, I wasn't even that curious about it, it was simply where I was going. It didn't seem a big deal, I mean it was a well trodden path.'

Thoughts of home

'IT WAS very, very weird. I used to wait until six o'clock, and any evening I could afford it, I used to run down to a telephone box without my husband knowing, and ring up my sister. I used to cry, I used to be so sick. The only people I spoke to were my babies, or when I went into the school or into a shop to ask for anything.'

*

'I THINK we've a fairly good sense of humour, and if it hadn't been for that I don't think we'd have lasted a week. I just went from day to day and apart from thinking of my mother and sister back home, I never gave anything else a thought.'

*

'I WAS lonely. To have lived in a small town where you just walk down the street and you know everybody, and then to be in London, in a hot July, at half past five in the evening, with thousands of people, and not knowing a soul, not knowing one person. I used to look at the Mooneys Irish House sign along High Holborn. It was the one familiar thing.'

Irish butchers' shop in Cricklewood, London

Irish provincial newspapers on sale in west London

From Dublin in the 1920s

They say you can't go back

Catherine Ridgeway has lived in England for sixty years. Here she reflects on the changes she has lived through.

I was born in the year 1905, in Dublin, and lived in Denmark Row. We were nine in the family altogether, but three children died in infancy, leaving three boys and three girls.

My grandmother ran a little vegetable shop and there were four rooms over the shop. My mother had two on the top floor and my grandmother had the bottom floor. I should think there were about fourteen families living in the Row and all of them had just two rooms. That seemed to be the norm. During the early period, my father worked as a cellar man. He joined the British Army in 1901 and served eight years and then came out on the army reserve. We used to rely on the reserve money to clothe ourselves. My mother served her time as a french polisher, then got married but with nine children she had plenty to do.

The Row was a long narrow little laneway and our water supply was from a fountain in the middle of the lane. Just on the right of it, was a long ramp down to three toilets because people had no toilets in their rooms. Nearly everybody had a bucket and the women used to be very embarrassed coming down with this bucket to the communal toilets. Invariably, they would go down with it either very early in the morning or late at night. It became infested with rats, so of course, they wouldn't go right down to the toilet, they'd just throw it down this ramp. The Public Health used to send people to swill it down with a hose about once a week! How they ever got away with it, I just don't know. I never saw a public health inspector there – ever!

And yet, some of the finest men and women came out of that Row and I'm often amused when I hear people talking about deprived children, because if ever children were deprived, we were. Yet, I never knew anyone who went to prison or was had up for stealing or anything like that. I don't know, we must have been a very placid lot.

I remember the Easter Rising[1] well because my mother and her sister were planning to go to Merrion Strand that day. My mother had five of us and my aunt had five and we'd go out on the train – a penny from Westland Row – with sandwiches and a teapot, and we'd park on the sands. We used to get our teapot filled with boiling water for a penny. On Easter Monday we were preparing to go and I remember going out into Henry Street and I saw men with bandeliers and guns in the windows of the Post Office. We got as far as the end of Henry Street when a policeman stopped us. When we said we were going to Westland Row Station, he said, 'Well, you're not going today. You must go back home and tell your mother the station is closed.' So we went back full of these men with their bandeliers and rifles – I think in those days they were known as the Volunteer Force. I had no idea what it was and I think the women in our family didn't have much time for it, as all the men were British soldiers you know. Anyway, the next thing was we heard shooting and we were confined to our Row by the police. We couldn't move out of it. And at night there were people running over the rooftops and we heard the shelling of the Post Office.

I remember one incident very vividly. We had a barricade with British soldiers at the bottom of Denmark Street, bordering on to Henry Street. A man got permission to walk down Denmark Street to attend to horses in his stable. And there was a whole crowd of men standing in our archway who kept peeping out and they stopped this man to ask him what was going on. But he'd been instructed by the troops to keep his hands up all the time, and the poor man dropped his hands as he spoke to them. A shot rang out and he was shot in the leg. I never saw anything like it. He went spinning round and round and then collapsed. So all these men who had been standing round fled, because they thought there was going to be more shooting and they left this poor man lying there. Then Miss Walsh, who used to run this little grocer's shop, came out and she got some of them back and they found a shutter and lifted him on to it. Someone put out a white flag and one of the policemen came down and arranged for him to be taken away. But I heard afterwards that he died a fortnight later because he'd lost so much blood. It was dreadful.

Then an officer came down and he rounded up all the men in the Row. All the women were weeping and wailing because they didn't know where they were taking the men. They were scared stiff. Anyway, it turned out that they only took them up to Dominic Street. They wanted them away from the Post Office area, you see, and they eventually evacuated us up there. People took us in, very kind they were. They gave us blankets and we lay down on the floor wherever we could. The Rising was pretty well over, coming up to the end of the week, and we were able to come back home again.

The next thing I remember was going out to see the damage. I remember climbing over a heap of rubble outside the Post Office and being shoved back again by the police. All the inside of the Post Office was gutted. It looked as if half O'Connell Street had gone, but actually it wasn't as bad as that. The Post Office got the worst of it for they shelled there and what shells didn't fall on it, dropped over to the other side. Never touched Nelson's Pillar!

I think most working-class people anyway, were sceptical of the Volunteers. Some thought they were traitors to act like that when thousands of Irishmen were in France fighting. Other people, of course, who wanted changes made in Ireland, independence for Ireland, took the opposite view. We heard about the executions and all that, but to me as a child between twelve and thirteen, it didn't mean a lot and I never heard my mother discussing it. Of course, I learned afterwards that it was a great tragedy. They really picked out all the men that they knew would cause trouble, had they been left alive. I think that is what it amounted to. My father was away at the time in the Great War, so was my uncle and my mother's brothers-in-law. In fact, we had five of them in that war. It was very common at that period, to have someone in the British Army and we never came into conflict with other families about it.

Then, in 1919, my father was posted to India and he took the whole family with him. I was thirteen then. We went to Jullundur, in the north, and we had our own little place and our own separate rooms which I enjoyed after the Row. My father served with the Connaught Rangers and while we were there, they had a mutiny.[2] It took the form of men downing tools because during that period, people in Ireland were having a bad time with the Black and Tans.[3] Mind you, it was kept very quiet. There was very few people in Ireland heard about it.

I went back to Dublin with the family in 1922 and I got work as a kitchen maid. But I was getting fed up with living in the Row. There was a factory at the back and they demolished two big huts which scattered a whole load of rats into our houses, and in the meantime, we'd developed bugs as well. I was seventeen and I was completely browned off with this. I woke up one night and saw a rat on the dressing table so that finished me off. I got the chance of a season job on the Isle of Man in a holiday camp. Then my aunt encouraged me to go to London, so I came in 1928. I think if my conditions had been better, I might not have left so easily, but you see, having been to India and having enjoyed a much better standard, there was no going back as far as I was concerned. I had to get permission from my father to leave – at the age of twenty-three! I'm amused at the way young people walk out now.

I thought London was a great place although at the time I was held back a bit because I had a bit of an inferiority complex about my small size and very little confidence. Nobody believes that now, but it was so at the time. I got a

Catherine Ridgeway at work, 1953/4

job as a chambermaid in a commercial hotel off Tottenham Court Road, stayed there a couple of years and then moved on to two or three other places, all chambermaid jobs. There were lots of Irish and Welsh girls in that type of work. I had to have somewhere I could live-in. I think that was the object of a lot of girls. It was another reason for so many nurses coming from Ireland, because it was just as difficult then to rent a flat or a room as it is today. So we all took jobs where you were assured of your bed and board.

Well, as a chambermaid, you'd be up in the morning about seven and you'd have to go around first with tea trays and then with jugs of hot water as there were no washbasins in small hotels at that time. Then you'd have your breakfast and when the guests came down, you'd have to go up and do the rooms. As well as doing the bedrooms, you might have the staircase to sweep down and dust and the bathrooms to do as well. You might have to help washing up in the kitchen and then a couple of hours off in the afternoon. But you'd be back again in the evening to lay out nightdresses and pyjamas and see that everything in the room was all right. You'd sit in the little service hatch and watch the bells to see if anybody wanted something. It would be about 9 o'clock at night before you'd finish. You'd have a half-day a week off and a half-day on Sunday, and the wages were ten shillings a week.

I never moved on unless it was for more money. Then I moved into a block of service flats. They were coming into being at the time because people with country houses wanted a flat in town. The conditions were better but you had long hours just the same. Now, I got my break by leaving the block of flats. I remember my uncle took me to one side, I was always grateful to him, and he said, 'You don't want to be a chambermaid till you're old, because they won't want you. You're deserving of something better. Why not try and get into the Linen Room as a linen maid or linen keeper. It won't be so hard as chambermaid's work.' So this is what I did and I was lucky. I got into the Oxford and Cambridge Club in Pall Mall. The linen keeper's job was to issue the clean linen to the chambermaids and send it out to the laundry. You checked it when it came in and did any repairs that had to be done. You assisted the housekeeper and when she was off-duty, took her place. I got £1 a week.

We had one very sad incident there. We had a couple of Irish sisters and one of them got pregnant. The man wanted to marry her but she wouldn't and her sister said to me, 'I'm getting out of here, because if she hangs on here, she'll drop it here.' Anyway, that's exactly what happened. One morning the girl got up and was dressed and packed and she was looking very, very ill. The housekeeper asked me to take her to some relatives in Kensington and say that she wanted medical attention. It was discovered afterwards that she'd had the baby and she said it never cried and never moved. She'd attended to herself and put the baby into a suitcase, and I'd carried the suitcase down! So, a week later a policeman turned up at work. It appears that the girl broke down in her friend's house and confessed about the baby. She had planned to go to Ireland and drop it over the side of the boat. She was charged, but she had a very humane man who defended her in court and she was put on probation. He said that she had already suffered her punishment. But the attitude then towards girls who got pregnant like that was very, very bitter. They didn't have much help. They had a hard time really unless they had sympathetic relatives or friends. That was why she didn't mention it to anybody.

During that period I didn't mix much with Irish people. Mostly English. I think my aunt and uncle put me off. They said, 'Don't get involved in Irish clubs or anything like that', because there was still the political background all the time. As the years went on and I was learning more about the political situation, I still didn't get involved, because you always had at the back of your mind that if anything crops up and you are involved, you might be deported or something like this. And I never wanted to leave London. I went home regularly, but I saw England as my home.

After I'd lived here for a while, I became very friendly with a man who opened up a new life for me and introduced me to good music, good literature, and walking holidays – in the Lake District, Ireland, Wales, anywhere you care to mention. We became very close. I think I've been in every city on the Continent for holidays. I also became active in 'Arms for Spain', demonstrating in Trafalgar Square for the opening of a second front. It all opened up a completely new life and gave me great confidence in myself.

In 1935, I had a job as linen keeper at the Waverley Hotel which included my own room. Oh, the joy of privacy after so many years of sharing rooms! The manageress was very kind and after a while she realised I was ambitious and suggested that if I was willing to spend some of my free time in the office learning book-keeping and typing, she would give me the next vacancy as their book-keeper and receptionist. This was my greatest break and I spent five happy years there. At the outbreak of World War Two I thought, this is my opportunity to get out of hotels, so I registered for government clerical work and got sent to work in the Assistance Board in Tottenham Court Road. The war gave me a break too, yes, I do feel that. I would never have got into the Civil Service in peace time. I wouldn't have had sufficient educational background, but because of the shortages, I got in. We were all employed as temporary staff – so that they could push us out when they didn't want us. And they started pushing us out in 1947. Mind you, they very much regretted it because they had trained us in on everything, widows' pensions, supplementary benefit, the lot. There were quite a lot of Irish working with the Assistance Board. You know, the only time I ran into comments about my nationality at that time, was at the Assistance Board. Another girl and myself had worked very hard on this section while the officer-in-charge was on sick leave. We were complimented by the boss, so we were very pleased. But this woman, who was the officer in charge, had a bit of a reputation as a martinet. You had to keep your head well down! So, one morning after she came back I was a bit late in setting out and when I got to the office I put out my work to show I was there and slipped off to the cloakroom. When I came down, this woman said, 'Miss Ridgeway, you're ten minutes late.'

'Oh no!' I said, 'I'm not late. You can see I've been here. I only slipped up to the cloakroom.'

Anyway, one word borrowed another and we didn't seem to agree about this.

She took me to the gentleman in charge of the whole section. She told her side of it and I burst out, 'We worked so hard to get everything up to date, and you take this attitude about five or ten minutes.' And she was a great big person and I was just a little person and she kept backing and I kept going forward, and he sat there and never said a word. Then he asked me to leave the room.

We were in the Civil Service Union there. I was always in the union, and we had a very good union secretary. She heard that I was going to be suspended

Catherine Ridgeway

through the typist who had seen a letter to the regional office. It said in the letter: 'Miss Ridgeway is of Dublin origin and therefore, inclined to be of a rebellious nature.' Well, I thought this was outrageous, because it had nothing to do with the argument at all, it was the first incident I'd been involved in and I'd been there a couple of years. Plus, she had a reputation for arguing with people. Anyway, the secretary went up to the boss and said, 'If anything happens to Titch (they always called me that) the whole office will down tools and we'll want to see the regional officer.' The letter was never sent.

I had never been shown any bias or nobody had ever mentioned the word Irish to me prior to that, in all the years I'd been around London in different jobs, and I was really incensed about it because it was really unjustified. I was the second Irish woman she'd come up against. I think we Irish are people who won't let them get away with anything, you know. We sort of defend ourselves very ably at times, especially if we think there is any bias.

After the war, when I went to work in housing, I often heard English people come into the office and, when nothing could be done for them, they might shout, 'Oh, the blacks, the Irish and all the aliens will be rehoused . . . I know someone who has only come over from Dublin and they're in a council house', but I wouldn't say anything. Sometimes, if I went into a house where I thought they were a bit biased, I wouldn't say I was Irish. Because the Liverpool and the Dublin accents are a bit similar, I have said, 'I come from Liverpool' where I thought there might be remarks. You had to protect yourself because you didn't want any rumpus.

But I loved the housing welfare officer's job. I was in my element going around visiting people and helping them, particularly when I went to East Barnet. I had my own office there and I would never have left only they started to amalgamate all the authorities and I lost my job. So I moved and got another housing welfare job in Lewisham. I was there for the last five years of my career. I retired in 1970 at the age of sixty-five.

Looking back over it, I suppose as a single woman you've more freedom. You've nobody to consider but yourself. You have your own money too – very important. I think my mother was very sorry I didn't marry. Well, she was of an older generation and it was of the natural order of things – you automatically married – wasn't it? I don't think I would ever have travelled so much if I'd been married. I'm sure I wouldn't. I would have been held down with the children. My uncle used to laughingly say, 'Oh, you might have been married in Dublin and have half a dozen children.' But you wouldn't have got very far with that lot, especially if the man wasn't wealthy. You have independence when you're single, I think that is putting it in a nutshell. It's a great advantage.

Notes

1. An uprising against British rule in 1916 by the Irish Volunteer Force – Headquarters were in the General Post Office in Dublin. Seven leaders were subsequently executed.
2. Mutiny in 1920 by Irish regiment in protest at Black & Tans atrocities in Ireland.
3. British mercenaries imported to fight against the IRA during the war of independence 1920–21. They mounted a campaign of terror against the populace at large. Their name came from the colour of their uniform and from the name of a well known pack of hounds in County Limerick.

Forty Years Away

Keeping the faith

A sense of history was crucial for Miriam James. Here, she talks about the difficulties of meshing this into her life in England.

Well, for the first twelve years of my life I was brought up in Scotland, in Dunfermline, Fife. In 1930, when my parents died, I went to Ireland and I was brought up by aunts and uncles, on the south side of Dublin. I was brought up a catholic, but I was never smothered as a catholic. My aunts were fairly religious, but it was a kind of secular religion, because they were very republican. I think the republican faith was very strong, and that acted as a sort of balance to an over-religious feeling.

I went to school in the city centre, Central Model Schools in Marlborough Street, because my mother had been there. My grandmother didn't like the local schools. It cost 5s 3d a term. It was a completely non-sectarian school – there were catholics, protestants and jews. The teacher I had was not a republican, but she was a really good nationalist – and I don't mean a chauvinist. She was a magnificent teacher, very good at inspiring people. She taught me more than anyone I've ever known. It was not so much what she taught me, but she taught me how to learn, and it was a remarkable experience. She got us a book to read, it was called *Rambles in Erin* by William Bulfin, and it was one of the first things that made me think seriously about Ireland. It was written just at the beginning of the Gaelic League,[1] and he explained why it was wrong that things British should be first in Ireland. When I read this I was at a very impressionable age – I was about fifteen, I suppose. It was obvious that I would have had a kind of republican faith anyway, because my uncle had been in the Four Courts,[2] and he was interned for four years, but I didn't know Ireland. It was this book, I think, that made me see what Ireland was, apart from Dublin. It made me realise that Ireland was a much bigger place, a much wider place both physically and spiritually than just the narrow confines of Dublin. It made me feel that Ireland was something to be proud of.

I didn't leave school till I was quite old for a kid of those days. They thought that I should be able to get a job in the Civil Service, which was considered absolutely wonderful. I didn't want to be in the Civil Service, being republican. I never wanted to work for the Free State, but again I felt I owed it to my aunts, who were very poor. My family thought it'd be a great job, and the head teacher in the school thought it'd be a good job. So they let me stay on at school until I was sixteen – until I could do the Civil Service exam – whereas normal kids of my age were taken from school at fourteen, and put to work in Jacob's Biscuit Factory, or something like that.

So, I started in the Civil Service when I was about seventeen. In the meantime, I did a holiday job for a month, which was running a playground in Foley Street. It was for very deprived children, and the vice president of Cumann na mBan[3] thought I'd be ideal for this job. I had joined Cumann na mBan already at this time.

I used to be there from four to six every day, to more or less teach the children how to play games, how to dance, how to play. They were kids who lived in these dreadful flats – they were really slums, and they needed something in their lives, something regular every day. But the playground was dreadful, indescribable. It was filthy. It was surrounded with corrugated iron and there was a little shed covered with corrugated iron, where the kids could go if it was raining. The little girls used to come into the hut with me, and the boys would sit on the roof and drum their heels on the corrugated iron. It was quite an experience.

I had joined Cumann na mBan when I was fourteen. Every Easter there used to be Cumann na mBan members – mostly – selling Easter Lilies. The Easter Lily, as you might know, is worn in remembrance of all those who have died for Ireland, in the same way as the poppy is the emblem of the dead for the British Empire. Well, I managed to get a box from someone who was on the executive of Cumann na mBan and go out selling Easter Lilies. She didn't realise I was quite so young, because I was very tall for my age. After, she said to me would I like to join, and I said 'Yes', of course. She said 'Have you anyone who could recommend you?' 'Well, my uncle was in the Four Courts, and he was in jail.' She didn't know him, but somebody did, and they let me in. I was the youngest member for a long time.

At that time we did fundraising for the republican prisoners, because there were always prisoners and prisoners' dependants. We also did a lot of education. You know, we held lectures on citizenship, civics it was called in those days, and history of course, because a lot of girls had not learned history

Miriam James

at school at all properly. They were in Cumann na mBan from conviction rather than from any knowledge. They were in it because they knew they were republicans, and they all had some sort of connection with the Republican Movement. We had political education and we used to meet and we learned military drill. That was about the most military thing I ever did in Cumann na mBan, I think. We used to parade. There were demonstrations, of course. There were always demonstrations, and meetings of various kinds. Easter Sunday there was always a big parade, and you were always in danger of being baton charged, or something like that, on Easter Sunday parade. And there was always Bodenstown;[4] that was the time you met everybody from all over the country. You met your friends that you might only meet once a year, at Bodenstown.

We ran céilís[5] and things like that for the prisoners' dependants and various good causes. At Christmas there was the Aonach na Nollaig, which means Christmas Fair. I sort of attached myself to Cumann na mBan head office, and that's where I learned typing and duplicating – I learned to type with one finger! Cumann na mBan and An Phoblacht newspaper offices were in the same building, and that's how I got to know people years older than myself. I suppose I was a nuisance, but I used to do the post, and go to the printers with seditious leaflets – things like that. I was very young. At the age of fourteen, fifteen, sixteen – even seventeen – you were still treated as a child in those days. You didn't learn anything that was important. Not that I would have wanted to. One of the things I was always taught was that you don't talk of anything you hear in here. When you're in here, anything you see or hear, you just don't say anything about. I mean, you just didn't.

Then came Republican Congress,[6] in 1934. Cumann na mBan was very much more left-wing inclined than perhaps the rest of the Republican Movement, apart from Saor Eire,[7] so myself and many other members joined. I felt that if the Republican Movement was to get anywhere, it had to begin with the poorest people. To show the poorest people, who seemed to form the majority of the population – they were the people we had to get round to believe in us – that a republic would be good for them. They wouldn't have such squalor and misery to contend with. Whether they were living in a republic or in an empire or the Free State, didn't mean anything to those people unless they had somewhere decent to live, and enough money to live on. And this was more or less what I believed the Republican Congress stood for. That it should not only be military, but it should have the socialist – well, we called it economic at that time, but I realise now that what we meant was socialist – that it should have the socialist side to it. So I was very happy to be in Republican Congress, and the Citizen Army which was resuscitated at that time. There was myself and Cora Hughes, and Eilis Ryan and Barbara McDonough. It was the first time in our experience that men and women were together in an army. We were all still in Cumann na mBan, but we were also in the Irish Citizen Army.

But that didn't last for very long – about six months. Because then came the break-up of Republican Congress when there was the question of whether it was going to be a political party, or whether it was going to be a united front. My family were a bit worried. They thought I was going to be drawn into communism, because although they weren't frantically religious, they were terribly afraid of communism – without being quite certain of what communism was. So they said that I could only be in Cumann na mBan. Of course, I was too young, I couldn't make my own choice. In those days you weren't allowed to make your own choice. People that I talked to said, well, at least you can do something in Cumann na mBan, so you might as well stay in Cumann na mBan, so I did. I never resigned from Cumann na mBan, so I could still be a member today!

It was during that time I saw the difference between the socialist side of the movement and the nationalist side, and that was one of the griefs, one of the sorrows, when the two sides didn't appear to be able to stay together. Well, it wasn't as clear as that, I suppose. It was just some people wanted to achieve a republic one way and others wanted to achieve it the other way. When Congress broke, it was a total split for a while, but then many people I knew drifted back into the Republican Movement again. I suppose I've always looked on the physical force movement as integral to the Republican Movement. It's a hard thing to say, because the idea of killing does not appeal to those who are in the Republican Movement. But if one looks back through history or looks at the history of the present day even, there would be no notice taken of any of the republican demands or republican statements if there were not the threat of physical force behind them.

There was a wilderness time for a few years because the people in Republican Congress had been so disillusioned – not only by the Congress splitting, but by the general feeling in the whole country. Indeed, throughout the whole of Europe there was this awful feeling of gloom. But the Spanish Civil War suddenly erupted. The more thinking people who were around Republican Congress realised that if they were genuine international socialists, here was something they could do about it. They were wise enough to see that there was something very nasty on the horizon, and they hoped perhaps by going to fight in Spain, that they might be able to make the rest of Europe wake up and see what was coming to them.

Girls were not particularly welcome in Spain, particularly girls of sixteen or seventeen as I was then, but a lot of my friends went. I knew all of the people from Dublin who went. The first boyfriend I ever had was killed in Spain. I knew most of them who were killed from Ireland. And while it was a time of sorrow, it was also a time of feeling, well, here was something that you could follow and that you could stand up for, that you could fight for and that you could do something about. We did a lot of publicity for the Spanish republicans, and we ran all sorts of functions for the Basque refugees, because there were quite a number of Basques in Ireland at that time. The Basque

Irish anti-facist poster, 1930s

FOR two years the people of Republican Spain have fought against the combined forces of Mussolini and Hitler.

Barcelona, Madrid, Bilbao, Tortosa and other centres in Spain. have suffered the horrors of air raids. Mussolini openly boasts that he is sending the airplanes, bombs and pilots responsible for the cruel warfare against the women and children af Republican Spain.

This is supposed to be a civil war. It is nothing of the kind. The Spanish people are fighting for liberty against a foreign Fascist invasion.

Frank Ryan, Republican fighter and leader of the Irish Unit, International Brigade, is now a prisoner in a Franco

jail. Italian officers control Franco territory and it is they who hold Frank Ryan prisoner. DEMAND HIS RELEASE!

The people of Dublin can extend no welcome to the warships of Mussolini -- the user of poison gas, the betrayer of Austria, the bomber of Spanish women and children and the jailer of Frank Ryan.

country was then fighting just as hard as it is now for its own separate identity.

All of this certainly accelerated my intellectual maturity – maybe not my physical maturity because I was very innocent in those days. I wasn't interested in men in the *slightest*. My family weren't particularly worried about what I did, so long as I was in at a respectable hour at night, that the neighbours wouldn't be talking – that was all that mattered! But I never looked on men as being anything but just other people who were in the movement. I was over thirty, I think, before I ever had an affair with anybody. I'd known men, been fond of men – but then I'd known women and been fond of women, so one was the same as the other as far as I was concerned. I wasn't interested. I wasn't conscious of being a woman, I was conscious of just being me! I had men friends, women friends, in fact I think I probably had slightly more men friends. The women friends I've had in my life I've been very close to, and count very, very dear, but I mixed with men slightly more than with women, as far as I can remember on a completely equal basis. I don't remember being counted out of anything because I was female. I had no sexual stirrings at that time at all, because my whole intellectual and my whole physical being was taken up with republicanism.

The last thing I ever thought of was getting married. I wasn't interested in it. I loved children, mind you, I'd fourteen young cousins, all much younger than myself. I took them to have all their injections in the hospitals, and when they were sick, took them to the doctor. That was one of the times I realised what being poor meant. In one of the families the father was out of work. And in order to get anything for nothing from the doctor you had to go to the dispensary and get a pink ticket, and then you'd get a green ticket to get your medicine free. And it was a very salutory experience, to be questioned as to why you didn't want to pay for what you were getting. It was probably one of the things that made me even more extremely socialist than I would have been otherwise, the way in which people were degraded by the questions they were asked.

Cumann na gCailíní[8] was going just about then, and I was involved. This was a junior organisation for Cumann na mBan, but it had a much wider reach, because little girls came to it from the age of about five. They weren't supposed to come till they were eight, but they were about five, and they came from not necessarily republican families. They came because Cumman na gCailíní was something different.

The first group I had was in d'Arcy's Hall in Donnybrook village. It's not there any more. Sheila Humphries and I had twenty, thirty kids there at different times. We did history lectures with them, we did singing, we did dancing. And I wrote a play for them, bringing in the poetry of William Rooney. We formed an Irish dancing troupe. There were quite a lot of branches of Cumman na gCailíní round the country, and we had competitions every year for them. They used to go to Bodenstown of course, and they used to go to all the demonstrations in Dublin.

I remember once we were marching down from Grafton Street, it was an evening demonstration, I think it was a hunger strike demonstration in the 1940s, and the demonstration was being baton-charged. And I was standing absolutely stiff with fright because I had these young kids behind me and I thought, 'My heavens, if the police come along and start baton-charging them, what am I going to do?' I wanted us to turn back, but the kids said, 'No, we're not going back. We're not afraid of the police. They won't knock us down, they wouldn't dare. We're not going back.' So I had to march them forward and safely out of the main procession. They weren't going to turn tail and run on the police.

Cumann na gCailíní was very good, because it was completely non-sectarian. There were a lot of non-catholic children. And it was all girls. It kept going until 1949, and now it has started up again. I've met quite a few of my cailíní the last few years I've been in Dublin, and they still remember the happy days. It was a light-hearted time. That was before the war.

I was working in the Civil Service all this time, and in their wisdom they decided to transfer me to Galway, heaven knows why. I must have been about three months there, I think, when I was arrested at work.[9] I was arrested on 27 June 1940. A date I'm never likely to forget, it was such a shock. That was when the IRA had more or less declared war on Britain and were taking the bombings to Britain, in the 1930s and 1940s. There were a few incidents in Ireland also. But I was very innocently going on with Cumann na gCailíní. I was in Cumann na mBan, obviously, and I used to go to their meetings. But I couldn't understand why I had been arrested. I'd just got to work. I worked in the employment exchange in Dominick Street and somebody rang over from the Claddagh exchange for me to go over there. I went over and the detectives were waiting to pick me up. They brought me to Dublin by car. They didn't even ask me any questions. I asked them where they were taking me and they said to Mountjoy Jail. I remember outside the gates of the 'Joy' when we got there, was Kit MacBride, who was Sean MacBride's wife. I said to Kit, 'Will you tell Louie that I'm here' – Louie being my aunt – 'will you tell her that I've been arrested.' I was astonished to find that there were thirteen other people there besides myself. I was the fourteenth. There was one kid from Galway whom I knew – why they didn't arrest the two of us together I'll never know. She was only sixteen I think. And there was one of the secretaries of Cumann na mBan and someone from An Phoblacht. It was really rather shocking. None of us had quite expected that women would be arrested. Loads of men had been interned, but it never dawned on us that they would intern women like this. I was doing absolutely nothing that could have merited being interned. I wasn't working with the IRA, I was only doing Cumann na gCailíní work.

I'm almost ashamed to say I was in prison when I think of what's happening in Armagh prison today, because we were never subjected to the indignities and the degradation that the girls in Armagh are subjected to. It was nothing like it. Being in prison in my day was like a holiday camp compared with what the people in Armagh are going through. We had political status, this was the difference. At first they tried to lock us into our cells, but there were three or four women with us who had been in prison previously in the 1920s, and they knew all the ropes. They knew exactly the demands we should be making – which was just as well, because I wouldn't have known. I was completely bewildered. In the back of your mind you always thought sometime or other you were going to be arrested – and what a great *heroine* you were going to be. You were going to stand up in court and declare that you didn't recognise the court, and everyone was going to think what a wonderful little heroine you were. But in actual fact, we were just picked up and dumped in the 'Joy', and there was one tiny little line in the national press, two lines I think it was, to say that women had been arrested from Galway and Dublin and Mullingar. So there was no honour or glory attached to it at all.

There was Sheila McInerney who was a wonderful person, and Fiona Plunkett who was the sister of Joseph Mary Plunkett who had been executed in 1916 – well, they'd been in before. They knew what to do, so we demanded that the only thing we should be deprived of should be our liberty. We should have free association at all times, which meant cell doors had to be left open. We had proper food, and we should have food parcels and books – all the demands that political prisoners make. It took, I suppose, about three weeks of arguments and fighting and refusing to go into the cells, and a few things like that, then they allowed us, and they left us more or less alone. They let us have classes. And the two Mulready sisters were marvellous because they were both musical. Kathleen used to play the harmonium and May, the fiddle. And we used to have great music – the other prisoners used to love it. They used to come in the morning and say, 'Oh, that was gorgeous last night. Oh, it was great listening to you last night.' Anyone who was in the 'Joy' during the period that we were there had free entertainment!

I was released on 20 March 1943, which made it two years and nine months, nearly three years. That was the equivalent of what I'd have done if I'd been charged and sentenced to four years' imprisonment. We were released gradually. Someone got out on parole because her mother was very ill. Then someone else got out for another reason. We could have got out at any time, if we were prepared to sign a form saying we wouldn't be connected with any more political activities. That was always there. You only had to go and say you were ready to sign, and that was it. You'd get out. But obviously no one was going to do that.

I remember it was on a Saturday that I was let out. I don't know whether I felt worse when I went in, or when I got out! It was just as strange walking outside the doors of Mountjoy as it was being put inside it. And they never used to warn you! The chief wardress just called me to the bottom of the stairs this Saturday morning and said, 'Go and get your things together.' I said, 'What do you mean?' 'You're out,' she said. Just like that! There were never any formalities about it at all.

The thing about coming out was that I couldn't talk to people. I missed the others. While we were in the 'Joy', the same as an enclosed group of people anywhere, you develop your own language, your own jargon. Nobody knew what I was talking about when I got out. It took quite a long time to learn ordinary everyday language again, a week or ten days to be able to talk to people without having to think what I was saying. And one was emotionally tied to the people who were inside, much more so than to the people who were outside, because your strings with the outside world had been cut completely. You lived in this small little cosy enclave which had nothing to do with the world in which there was a war raging.

I wandered around Dublin just trying to get used to being there again. People all wanted to see me, people that knew me, and my aunts' friends and my friends from the Civil Service who had been extremely good in coming to see me, and sending in parcels and that. Eventually, the Civil Service wrote to me offering my job back, if I was prepared to go to Mullingar. I didn't want to, because it meant I had to sign that while I was employed by the Civil Service I wouldn't be involved in Cumann na mBan. Then people like Sheila Humphries and a few more people I knew said, 'Look you're doing no good hanging around. Your family need money.' It was very difficult, but then, it was the fact that my family really was very poor and that at least I'd be able to give them some money. So, I went back to the Civil Service after about three months and only worked with Cumann na gCailíní until I went to London in 1949.

I remember the last Saturday I was in Dublin, I took the cailíní on a tour of Scoil Eanna – Padraig Pearse's[10] school. His sister was still alive then, and she showed us through all the rooms and told us various things about the two Pearses when they were little boys. I don't think I'd recognise Scoil Eanna now, it's been turned into a museum, I think. It was still a home then. Senator Margaret Pearse lived there, and it was a very special thing that she allowed Cumann na gCailíní to go round. I think then we had a picnic in the grounds after that. That was my last conscious political act in Dublin.

I left Dublin without telling anyone I was going. No one knew I was going. I left because of a secret affair with a married man, no other reason at all. Later on I let people know I was still alive and kicking – I sent money home, but I never gave anyone my address. I just couldn't have coped with the emotional upsets of that particular period. I couldn't have faced the weepings and wailings. That's why I didn't go back home for donkey's years.

When I came to London first I thought it was completely without a soul. I looked at people's faces and they lacked any sort of spiritual quality which I'd been used to seeing in Irish people's faces. That's what I thought then, but I realise now that they were people who were just recovering from the trauma of the war. I was very much aware of there having been a war, particularly walking through the London streets and seeing the bomb sites which were eyesores in some parts of the city, and in other parts had been turned into gardens. But it was the emptiness of people's faces, the lack of mobility of people's faces that I found very strange when I came here. People didn't smile as readily as they did at home. It was the closed-in faces that I came across here that surprised me most and that made me feel most uncomfortable. When I met people they were always very nice, but there was always this reserve, and it wasn't because I was Irish, the reserve would have been there with anybody. It was amongst themselves, I could see it.

When I came to England I shut up about politics. As I came here because I wanted to, I felt I didn't have the right to talk too much about politics. But I did miss it, because politics had been very much part of my living until then. I felt it very much. The Irish attitude is that everybody has something to say about politics. They may not *do* anything, but they'll certainly take up a political attitude, but in England, people don't. If you talk about politics, or anything that they think is political, they'll shy away from it. I found this dozens of times, even with anti-apartheid agitation. They just feel that anything that is, or appears to be, anti-establishment is politics, and they don't want anything to do with it. In trade unions there are so many items that can't be brought up on the agenda, or discussed, because they are deemed political.

I also realised that there wasn't any interest in Ireland from a political point of view. Ireland was more or less dismissed as being of no account – which in the aftermath of the war was understandable. I did have a lot of arguments with people about Ireland not being in the war. People couldn't understand why Ireland couldn't see the cause of Britain as being their cause. They couldn't see in any way that Ireland had any right to separate itself in its policy from Britain. Obviously, they had never been taught anything about Irish history, and they were completely unaware of the role that Britain had played in Ireland.

It's the one thing that has always failed me – I've never been able to hold an intelligent conversation about Ireland with an ordinary, unpolitical English person. Because we just don't speak the same language at all. But, when I came here first I didn't want to be involved in politics because I was coming, as I said, as a sort of guest. I didn't want to get involved in deeply republican things at that time, because I felt it wouldn't be the right thing to do. I thought I'd be going back to Dublin in a couple of years' time. You see, I never envisaged staying here for ever and ever.

I remember the first job I got here. After a while I learned to operate the switchboard and I used to relieve the girl that was on the telephone, but the boss didn't like my accent, so I wasn't allowed to answer the telephone any more. I had been in the job about three or four years, but he didn't like the idea of having an Irish accent at the end of his telephone. Most of his customers and his friends seemed to like talking to me, but I think he thought it wasn't good for his image to have an Irishwoman on the telephone. That was the first occasion on which I was rejected as an Irish person, and it was a very salutory lesson. I didn't like it. I was very annoyed and I did complain. 'What's wrong with my voice?' I spoke perfectly good English, I was perfectly polite, and I was reassured – 'Oh no. It's nothing like that. It's just your accent. Mr Sweetman doesn't like your accent.' After that I left, in 1954. I felt I needed a change. I had various jobs, and then I worked for the BBC news service until I retired in 1983.

My first return to Dublin was about thirty years after I left. In 1979 I read in *The Irish Post* that the remains of Frank Ryan[11] were being returned to Dublin for burial, or reburial. He had died in Germany after being taken there from prison in Spain, during the war. I thought, well, I would very much like to go to the reinterrment, because he had been one of my great heroes when I was a young one. It wasn't just hero worship. I knew him, and had admiration and a great liking for him. So overnight I decided to go to Dublin.

As the boat went into the harbour I didn't know what to feel. In a sense I was rather dead. I was looking at the Sugarloaf and looking at the mountains, the Dublin mountains and the Wicklow hills, and in a sense I felt dead, and in another sense, the words of a song my mother used to sing came back to me – they always do – looking at the dawn on the hills of Ireland.

> And Ireland isn't it grand you look
> Like a bride in her rich adorning
> And out of my very heart of hearts
> I bid you the top of the morning.

I got there, and I booked a room in the Pillar Hotel. I was just sitting listening to the radio, having my breakfast in this hotel, having come straight from the boat, when it said on the radio that the funeral of Frank Ryan would be that very Friday morning. The press had said that the burial would take place on the Saturday. So I had to rush, change and get myself up to Whitefriar Street Church in Dublin, and I really felt like death, after coming over on the boat, and the high emotion that it aroused in me to be back in Dublin again, and the reason I was there. So I just went. Went to the church, and I found it very moving to see his coffin before the altar, draped in the Tricolour and the Spanish flag. I recognised a few people, not very many. And nobody at first saw me. A couple of people smiled at me and I didn't know whether to talk to them or not. Anyway, I got a taxi to Glasnevin and went with the cortège to the graveside, and I saw Frank's sister. I went over and she said, 'Who is it?', because she was very frail at the time, and I said, 'It's Miriam, you probably don't remember me.' 'Oh, Miriam James,' she said, so I knew she remembered me. The next day, there was a commemoration for him in Glasnevin, and I went to that. And a whole lot of people came up and

A protester at a hunger strike demonstration in London, 1983

spoke to me at that. The word had got round that I was back. I stayed only till Sunday night. I had to come back to work on the Monday morning, but I've been going back regularly since then.

I was a whole mixture of feelings about going home. The fact that it was Frank Ryan, that I was going back for his funeral ... thinking back on the days when he was around, and the sort of heady days of the Spanish Civil War, before the Second World War ... There were so many emotions that not one of them had full rein, because it was too much.

I was in no political organisation in England until the end of the seventies. I felt that British political organisations had nothing to do with me. I was holding myself for whatever might happen in Ireland. In the back of my mind there was always the feeling, and I always hoped that perhaps some use might be found for me there. And I think that is the main reason I withheld myself from the British political scene for so long.

It was about 1977 that I first became interested in local politics and became involved in community activities here. I'd always been conscious of the fact that there was harassment of the Black community around where I live, and I always wanted to stand up and be counted with those who were standing with the Black community. But that wasn't very easy, because one could be looked on as an interloper and somebody who was a do-gooder, which is about the last thing one ever wants to be known as. Then I happened to be at a meeting where some people were suggesting that the West Indian people in All Saints Road should sort of be cleared out – not in so many words obviously, but this was the imputation of their remarks. I was so infuriated at the way these people were talking, I stood up and said what I thought. Some other people did as well, and I was asked then to go on the working party for the general improvement area in this part of Notting Hill. From then on I suddenly found myself head over heels into the middle of local politics.

Along with all this I was obviously interested in Ireland, because from 1969 onwards the situation in Ireland had taken a new turn. It was plain to see what was going to happen, so I was keeping my eye on that while I was interested in politics here. None of the parties here seemed to understand what was going on in Ireland. They didn't understand what was going on with the Black community, never mind what was going on in Ireland. So, side by side, militant black groupings were coming together in Britain, while militant Irish groupings were making their presence felt in Ireland and in Britain. I was asked to join the Labour Party and I refused over and over again. Then I became aware of the Labour Committee on Ireland, and I joined the Labour Party in December 1980, or January '81 – I couldn't give you an exact date. I applied to join the Labour Committee on Ireland, but it wasn't till June 1983 that I succeeded, and immediately was asked to be secretary of the regional group!

Of all the parties here I think the Labour Party is the only viable party for a socialist. And a few people in the Labour Party make the right sort of statements about Ireland. I began to feel that I was doing something, however little, making some progress towards moving people into thinking about

Ireland. The Labour Committee on Ireland has certainly started a very strong and worthwhile dialogue with the republicans in Ireland, both in the Six Counties and the Twenty-six Counties. So I feel very enthusiastic about it now, because I feel that I can do something worthwhile even while living in London. Working in ordinary British politics was a safety valve, but it was very important to get back into doing something I felt was reactivating other people's interest in Ireland, and perhaps making them think about Ireland, and making them think differently.

Looking to the future – first of all, have we got a future? Are Reaganism and Thatcherism going to put an end to our futures? I think that the anti-nuclear campaign is one of the most important things that has been in our life in the past fifteen years, and is one in which women have played a remarkable part. CND has its faults, but nevertheless it has restored hope to a lot of people who feared for their own and their children's futures. That is one of the most horrible thoughts that one of my age takes on looking into the future. That it is my generation principally who has been responsible for the despoliation of the planet. We have demanded more and more and more of the goodies of the earth, and not cared about the rest. Perhaps the younger generations may decide that this isn't the heritage that they want to pass on to their kids. Sounds very grandiloquent I know, but it's something that eats at one's heart by times. When you read about famines and disasters and think that we in this part of the world live so well. There's not much we can do about it individually, but the guilt I'm afraid is on us.

It makes me feel very sad, by times, because I think that if I had stayed in Ireland, I could probably have done something. And then I think again, no, I don't think I could. Because Ireland is tinged with the same selfishness, only in a different way. It's true that so many Irish people who had worth, who had goodness, and who had the potential of even greatness, left Ireland. It became a fashion, almost a necessity to do so. Because Ireland had been drained not only of wealth, but of self-respect. They couldn't prove themselves in Ireland, and you had to go away in order to regain your own self-respect. This is the legacy of colonialism, and you find it in all the other colonised countries too.

Miriam died in December 1986, about a year after this interview. She was active in politics until her death. Her generosity and enduring courage are an inspiration to us and we are proud to be able to share some of her story with others.

Notes

1. The Gaelic League was founded in 1893 to revive interest in and everyday use of the Irish language. It led to a revival of interest in Gaelic music, dancing, arts and crafts.

2. One of the strategic public buildings in Dublin occupied by the republicans during the 1916 Rising and occupied by anti-Treaty forces during the Civil War.
3. Cumann na mBan was the women's army of the Irish Volunteers. Founded in 1914, it grew very quickly and the members were actively involved in struggle for many years.
4. Every year republicans and socialists gather at Wolfe Tone's grave at Bodenstown.
5. A céilí is a traditional Irish dance.
6. In early 1934 there were calls for a Republican Congress to rally all shades of socialist, republican and anti-fascist forces in Ireland, North and South. The movement gained momentum and after months of organising branches existed in many areas, a regular newspaper was produced, and the Irish Citizen Army was briefly revived. Republican Congress was held on 29/30 September 1934, but split on the contentious issue of whether it should become a new revolutionary socialist party. It continued in a reduced capacity and in 1936 became the rallying ground for anti-Franco forces and support for Spanish republicans, and was involved in organising the Irish Battalion of the International Brigade. With the fall of the Spanish republic, the organisation became inactive.
7. A movement formed in 1931 to unite the working class and working farmers against British imperialism and Irish capitalism.
8. Cumann na gCailíní was the junior organisation of Cumann na mBan.
9. At this time many republicans were interned.
10. Padraig Pearse was one of the signatories of the 1916 Proclamation and was executed by the British as a result. He founded an Irish speaking school in Dublin.
11. Frank Ryan was a republican who led the Irish Battalion of the International Brigade in the Spanish Civil War. He was captured and taken to Germany, where he remained a prisoner until his death in 1944. His body was returned to Ireland in 1979.

Language and Culture

Threads of a garment

Brid Boland is a traditional singer who has lived in London for six years. She talks about her musical heritage.

The area of County Sligo where I was born is known as Michael Coleman country – he was a fiddle player who had emigrated to America. It was a very rich area for fiddle and flute music but particularly fiddle music. There's people who say that at one time you could hand the fiddle round at a local church and anybody could play it. That's mostly gone now, but South Sligo is still one of the areas that's very rich in that sort of tradition.

There was a lot of emigration from there, especially to America – New York, Chicago, Ohio – and there's a whole host of musicians who emigrated. It really affected the music, because so many of the emigrants were musicians. It was a big blow to Irish cultural life, and it took its toll. It took away morale, people leaving, and demoralised those left behind. Many of the musicians who left were recorded in America, although some would say there were even better musicians that stayed behind but their music was lost because it was never recorded.

When I was growing up in the 1960s, that part of Ireland was very rural and a lot of the social life took place in people's houses. There were lots of people who played – my mother's cousin was a really nice fiddle player and there were other women who played. My mother, I thought, was a really nice fiddle player. She had been taught by her father. She used to play the fiddle in the house; we'd ask her to play, or sometimes we had parties in our house. There were winters when there used to be a spate of parties – that was in the early 1960s when there was a sort of revival. I suppose some older people thought the tradition was dying out. There were a few of them who started to revive the interest in Irish music around the area, so a lot of children went off to learn dancing and to play instruments as well. We were encouraged to play as children and we were battering away at tin whistles at an early age. I grew up in that kind of environment, where music was very prominent, and I consider it a rich part of my background.

In the 1970s though, the popularity of pubs and the new big lounge-bars had a big influence on the culture. Before that, music wasn't usually played in pubs, it was played in people's houses most of the time. Then, I think, a change happened. People started going out to the pubs and the lounge-bars and they started having music in them. A lot of the women stopped playing, including my mother and a lot of other women I knew, because the scene where women had been recognised had broken down. The people who played in the pubs were mostly men. I think the Irish music scene is dominated by men, and it's mostly men who play the instruments.

When I first left Ireland, I went to live in Denmark for six months, and it was there that I first began to develop an awareness of what being Irish meant to me, how I was different and why I was different. I suppose I felt, for one thing, it was a different way of communicating or a different understanding with other Irish people. Even with Irish people from different backgrounds, there is still some common way of understanding, of communicating, which is an unsaid thing, and which is very hard to try to describe in words. Often it's something to do with the way somebody talks, or the sound of the voice. Irish people's voices sound different, the tone with which they speak is different and it expresses something that's different. It's like expressing some part of a soul. Also, the English that Irish people speak is built on translations from the Irish language a lot of the time like, 'I'm after coming in . . .'. I think the destruction of the language is devastating, because it is the use of symbols, something that the people built up over thousands of years and developed as a way that they would relate to each other, communicate with each other, and then that was just destroyed. It's a massive blow to destroy the common usage of symbols between people.

I know that a lot of people didn't have an interest in Irish music before they left Ireland and they started developing it then. Somehow or other it seems that music goes beyond words, that it is easier to tap as a way of identifying what your difference is, and it expresses something that is very personal to you. Probably it could be done in other ways, through poetry or art or something, but it seems like music is easier. I think it's part of the whole thing of becoming aware of what being Irish is, which you don't realise until you're placed in a situation which forces you to find out.

When I first came to London, six years ago, I lived in Kilburn. I was interested in what the Irish community was like over here, and I thought it might be quite nice to be there. But I felt I really hated Kilburn – it seemed depressing to me. The first weekend I arrived in London I went to Biddie Mulligans pub, and I remember this man being grossly insulting to me at the counter when I was ordering a drink, and I thought, 'My God, this is my first experience of the Irish community here.' But I also got a lot of kindness from other Irish people. I felt I wanted to get out of it though, and that it placed the exact same confines on me as if I were still in Ireland. After I'd been here a while, I met some Irish feminists and that changed my whole life. There seemed to be a whole community of Irish people who were socialist feminists in Islington, in North London. They'd emigrated from Ireland in the 1970s and a whole different dimension had developed. That's what I was interested in, and I moved over to that side of London. These women gave me the space and the environment to explore what I wanted. They were interested in Irish culture, and there was a whole different little Irish world going on there – much more than in Brent, which really surprised me, because Brent has such a huge Irish community.

I didn't sing then, I just sat and listened. I developed my feminist politics through the Irish women's movement here, and it was Irish women friends who encouraged me to sing – most definitely it wasn't the straight Irish music scene. It's still very much a male preserve and it's often quite hard for women in sessions to develop their confidence, and to be assertive enough to just jump in there and play, regardless. I know a few women who would be capable of playing in sessions, but they don't have the confidence to go in there, and they're at a standard where they could actually join in.

I sing now in a band called the Sheelas. In 1986, for International Women's Day, the big band Sheela na Gig came together and performed for maybe six or seven events which were on for the month of March. But it was very difficult keeping everyone together, there was such a diversity of women in the band, so it disintegrated. There were five of us who decided to keep going. That's how the Sheelas formed, and we've kept going since then. It's very enjoyable. It's quite hard work and time-consuming, and with me, because I'm the singer in the band, I find it very frustrating. I can't write songs, and I feel very confined in the sort of songs I sing. I find it hard to develop. I'm probably the most frustrated person in the band for that reason.

There's a huge problem with the singing, in that it doesn't express my experience as a woman. It's written mostly from a male perspective. The images of women in the singing are very limiting and often derogatory. For instance, I don't know of any positive image of older women – they're all 'hags' or 'crones', with the male interpretation of those words, and the young women are '*femmes fatales*'. They aren't celebrated at all in nationalist songs or else they're portrayed as victims or elevated to being identified with their country. That needn't be negative in itself, except that it's the only image of women in the surviving tradition. Generally, one never gets a sense of what women felt – it's supposed to be contained within the male experience. It makes me feel quite angry that the history of women has been lost and ignored and denied. I mean, all of the women who've fought for Irish freedom, and they've never been celebrated, never had a song written about them.

It also seems that women haven't had access to the song-writing tradition. I don't know whether songs have been lost, or whether they just didn't write them. But there's a whole huge gap. So it seems like women have to go back and pick up those pieces and write new things, to bring back to life a tradition that has been buried. And yet, it's hard to do that – like picking up fragments that have been left behind. It feels to me like you hold the threads of a garment and the rest of the garment is lost or burnt and there's just bits left in the fire, and you have to try and pick them out and piece them together. This is particularly difficult since the history of folk culture has been an oral one and in the case of Ireland, the greater part has been destroyed by colonialism.

So, it's very limiting as a woman singer, and yet it seems a pity to abandon the singing because the actual structure, the melodies and the way you can use your voice, seem a lot more important than the words. The sound expresses so much more above and beyond the words. I think the sounds used in a lot of Irish traditional songs have reached the level of being classics. It's not just that they express the real soul of Ireland but some of them reach something that's universal, maybe in the same way that an Indian mantra will. It's to do with the sounds rather than the words.

In the Sheelas everybody really enjoys working together, and I'd like to keep it as a women's band because it has a very special flavour when it's women only. Everybody in the band really wants to play, but they do want to gain recognition. We're tapped into a market at the moment where until recently there has been a gap. I suppose that's a development in the women's movement here generally, as well as in left-wing Irish politics, that women's bands have become quite popular. It's about affirming women's music – women and Irish music. I think Irish music expresses a part of me that couldn't be expressed in any other way. I think there's an emotional and spiritual fulfilment that comes from it. I find it very therapeutic, I suppose, partly because it's expressing something I couldn't imagine not being able to express. I suppose it's something to do with being Irish and it's an emotional and spiritual nourishment. I wouldn't choose to go back at this moment and live in Ireland, but I go back every year, and go to music festivals and listen to a lot of music and I am replenished, renourished through it, in a way that going anywhere else on holiday wouldn't do . . . couldn't do.

I couldn't imagine leaving the music behind when I emigrated. I mean it would be such an extreme deprivation, and it would be like denying a really big part of myself. Most of the Irish culture here is still based on the same themes as in Ireland. There isn't a song-writing or a singing tradition that is based on being an immigrant in this country. The songs seem to be mostly about leaving home, there isn't much about living here. It could be the proximity of Ireland. A lot of Irish people live here all their lives and they never intended to, they keep dreaming of going back and the years just pass. But I think the Irish community is beginning to develop a separate identity in this country now, but it really depends on second generation Irish to affirm their Irishness, and draw from that tradition, and express that experience.

The annual Irish festival at Roundwood Park, Brent

A woman doing her daughter's hair at a dancing feis

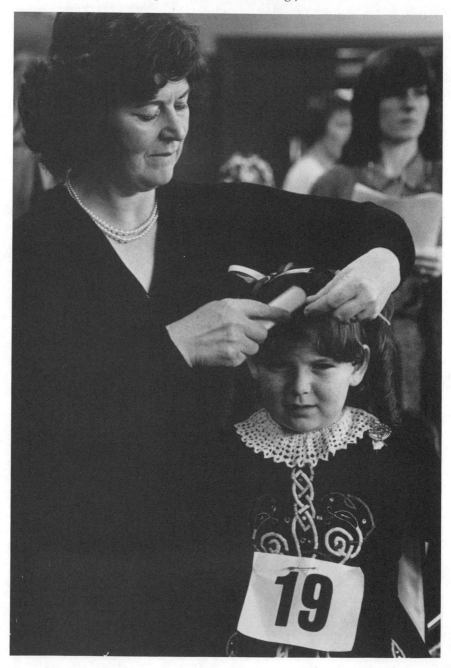

Irish bookshop, London

Opposite: An Irish dancing competition in Croydon
Below: A woman and parish priest after Sunday Mass

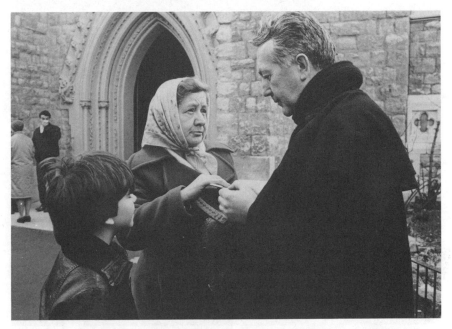

Below: Dancing display at the Roundwood Irish Festival

Siobhan Uí Neill teaching Irish language at an adult evening class

Céilí dancing at the annual festival at Roundwood

Singing at a social to commemorate the hunger strikers, London, 1983

82

Opposite: Going to a dance on a Saturday night at the National Club, Kilburn
Below: Camogie

Country and Western music lovers at the Roundwood festival

Playing in the parade at the Roundwood Festival

Getting ready for a camogie match

St Patrick's Night dance at the Camden Irish Centre

At the second Irish Women's Conference, London, 1985

a new language
is a kind of scar
and heals after a while
into a passable imitation
of what went before.

Eileen Doherty, a schoolteacher in Brent, discusses how language and culture embody a people's sense of themselves.

Language plays a very central part in one's image of oneself. It has a very important role. It adds another dimension and goes a long way towards understanding our heritage. The loss of the language for the Irish people means that it's an impoverished culture. Our culture is impoverished in the sense that it's a restricted culture. I suppose that is what has made the English people so self-assured and confident . . . their language is used throughout the world. There's a West Indian poet called Braithwaite and he talks about 'nam' the naming, you know, what's in a name? He goes back to African influences in the Caribbean dialects and how important it is to have your own name for things, your own 'nam'. Your language gives you that basic confidence in yourself, in your roots. You have a means of communicating with your own people which goes back and links you with your past generations.

I was born in Rosguill, a Gaeltacht[1] area in north west Donegal; it's a very beautiful peninsula, you have an area there which is known as the Atlantic Drive with lovely beaches, so we get quite a lot of tourists. The tourist industry was there long before the rest of the country with a lot of English tourists who could afford to buy second homes. And that had quite a bearing on the place because although the peninsula as a whole was Gaelic speaking, some of the little villages were English speaking. So you had a change to English much sooner and more rapidly than you would have expected otherwise. It's the legacy of tourism that people would bend over backways to speak English as opposed to in the large Gaeltacht in Gweedore where the people were very proud of their Gaeltacht. I remember that where I came from, they used to refer to people from Gweedore as being very stroppy. In Gweedore, shopkeepers would expect you to converse in Irish and very few concessions would be made.

My own family was not from the area – my father was from Derry City and my mother was from another part of Donegal. My father inherited a business in the area, a general shop, which he'd worked in as a young man. He was interested in Irish, learned it and he'd have spoken it but not quite with the right *blas*.[2] It would have been obvious that he wasn't a native speaker, though the Irish would have been good. I remember as a small child, my neighbours saying to me, 'Oh, you speak Irish just like your father,' and that wasn't a compliment! It would be the *blas*, the actual intonation, it wouldn't be exactly as they had it. Both my parents were committed to Irish and certainly they encouraged the children to speak it. So, we all inherited a lot of respect for the language. But my mother died when I was thirteen months. I was the youngest of four and my aunt came to live with us and she was totally opposed to Irish. So, you had two very opposing traditions in the house as I was growing up. The children used to use it as a subversive language.

I certainly had a complex about the language. I had no problems learning to read it, but speaking it certainly did something to my confidence. I remember sitting in the classroom rehearsing over and over again, 'Bhfuil cead agam dul amach, a mháistir?'[3] because although I knew it, I lacked confidence to actually say it. It just goes to show how children are conditioned ... I don't think I had difficulty communicating or that my grammar was imperfect, it was just the label I had, that I was not a native speaker, and therefore I couldn't perform as well as the others. When I think about the pupils I teach now and the arguments against streaming, I think about that. You know, I think my Irish would have been quite good, it was just that I imagined it wasn't because it shouldn't be.

Looking back on it, there wasn't much help from the Irish government to keep the language alive. Because of our geographical location, we really were much closer in spirit, and in many other ways, to the North of Ireland and I suppose we expected very little from the Southern government. Just as well, as we got very little. And you know, the emigration from that part of the country kept the rest of the population there. It was mainly to Scotland and England; the emigration to America had really gone down to a trickle by the mid-fifties but a lot of people had relatives in America and they got legacies and clothes from these relatives. I used to see the Yankees coming home. I have lots of memories of that.

The only form of subsidy that the Gaeltacht people got at that time was the Irish speaking grant. It was like a hand-out for living in the Gaeltacht, but in order to get the grant, you had to prove that you spoke Irish all the time. I was the only one who hadn't got the grant in our house. The master would have informed the *cigire*[4] of the fact that my aunt didn't speak Irish at home ... your supergrass! Yeh, one could feel bitter about it, the master knowing full well my father's attitude to Irish and how the circumstances had changed within the family. You know, it was quite a mean trick. Without the grant, I couldn't enter for the scholarship and the two youngest were dependent on scholarships to go to secondary school. I got it when I was eleven and it's just dawned on me now that the reason that the master recommended that I receive this Irish grant was because I was the only one who got the scholarship, eventually. The teachers were very competitive and I suppose it was in his interest that I should be entered for the scholarship.

Now, I'll tell you something else about that. When it came to the scholarship exam, we had to get something like 80 – 90 per cent in the oral Irish. And I remember the master pointing to two of us in the class beforehand and he said, well, I wouldn't get one because I didn't have any Irish and my friend wouldn't get one because she wouldn't speak! So it came to the oral and the two of us were examined at the same time and I spoke throughout. I didn't wait for questions or I hardly waited for questions. If I saw a bird passing at the window, I brought that into the conversation as I went along. And the person being examined alongside me who was a native speaker, spoke no English at home, replied 'Yes' and 'No' to everything and I remember thinking, even then, 'My God, this is unfair!' It was a very competitive system.

Up till that stage, I hated Irish. My sister next to me made me speak it when we were playing. She had a natural gift for it. In fact, she used to make a great impression on the *cigire* and at times he'd wonder where she got her vocabulary from, because he hadn't heard some of the words. His Irish wouldn't have been that good. But I was very competitive then and I realised that the people from the village who didn't speak Irish at home, all had plenty of money, so they weren't dependent on scholarships as a means to advancement. I was in the position where I had to be. The better-off people all spoke English – absolutely. But when I went to school in Dublin, I suddenly realised that I had very good Irish and it changed my attitude overnight. I went to Scoil Catríona on the scholarship and after that to Galway University where I studied mainly through Irish.

I came here in 1974. I thought I'd have a year in London and my eldest sister had a house here. Within a couple of days I got a job, supply teaching in Brent and if I were to point to any single factor for keeping me in London, it was my very early weeks in England. It was an all-girls school, a very rigid set-up. The book stock was totally inadequate for mixed ability teaching and I was left with these classes – the sixth and seventh stream from the top. I had never come across slow learners or disruptive pupils before. It was such a shock to my system that I'm sure I've never fully recovered from it. You were totally aware that the kids were learning very little. I had almost a guilt complex about it which I suppose determined my stay in London.

It was also my first experience of being Irish outside of Ireland. That was something I hadn't really thought about because I felt so positive about my identity. I didn't expect anyone to regard me as different in an inferior sense. There was an Irish chap at that school so we used to speak quite a lot in Irish, in the staffroom, regardless of who was there. I remember a month after I arrived, a girl in my form being a bit silly and a co-tutor turning to me and saying, 'Isn't that a very Irish thing for her to do.' I was appalled. That was my first experience of a negative attitude towards Irish people. The English people I had met in Rosguill liked Ireland very much, appreciated what it had to offer and I was totally unprepared for the ordinary English person's perception of Irish people. You see, I kept the historical relationship that we had with England in one compartment and I was really aware of that, but the actual day-to-day contact with English people was a shock to me when I met up with it. When people spoke about Ireland, I expected them to know something about Irish culture, writing, scenery or whatever. And I'm sure it took me some time to realise that what I was hearing was the average English person's attitude to Ireland. They have an ethnocentric approach and anything outside of their own culture they regard as either inferior or exotic.

I have never really adjusted to it but it took me a while to even come to terms with it. Some people here aren't even aware that there is an Irish language. Now, ten years on, I'm quite aggressive about it all. I wouldn't ever describe myself in 1974 as being aggressively Irish, but I was certainly very confident and very positive. But it's something I should reflect on a little bit. Does one have to be aggressive about it? Is that inevitable? I suppose in my case that's the way it has developed. I have never let an 'Irish joke' go by. I'd never accept it. I've made my position very clear on that.

I had to take a stand on this a few years ago. A play was being rehearsed in the school and one day while covering a class I asked a pupil to show me a copy of the play, which she was reading. I was horrified at what I saw – the 'Paddy' character was one of the worst examples of the stereotyped image of the Irishman I've yet to see. I was told, 'Oh, when you see the whole play in context, you'll understand.' I got a copy of the play and discovered that the whole thing was just based on stereotyping – there was a take-off of an Indian boy, a Chinese, velly this, velly that and you had the sexist, racist interpretation of the Russians and the all-American hero. I was appalled . . . and our school had a reputation for multicultural education!

When I first objected to it, I suppose I thought it could be amended. It was my first experience of this sort of thing and I didn't realise at this stage that I would have to stop the play. I mean the thought of stopping a play that has been in rehearsal for a long time – the money, costumes, staff involved! But it became apparent that once you do take a stance, you know, you have to see it through. When I'd pointed out that it was based on stereotyping, it came back to me that, 'Yes, there was stereotyping, but they were making a send-up of it.' So I pointed out that programmes which do adopt that line have no effect on people who are racist. The union representative came to see me and said that the people staging it were threatening me with unprofessional conduct on the grounds that I had discussed it with the children, so the atmosphere in the staffroom was really quite hostile. There were eighty staff and four were actively supporting me. Eventually, the headmaster silenced me and said he was going to send a copy of my complaint to the borough's multicultural advisor.

I was certainly very worked up because although I had this reputation for stirring things up, I still like a tranquil atmosphere and it was very difficult working in that atmosphere. So, the advisor wrote back a very good letter to the Head but the Head never showed it to me nor told me the consequences. The kids came to me and said, 'Our play can't go on because you didn't like the Irish character in it.' I was a bit sad because those kids knew I was interested in drama too so they would have had divided loyalties. I saw the letter and it said that he didn't understand why the issue raised itself in the first place because the school was committed to a multicultural approach and that stereotyping was not the way to go about it. He also said that what I did was unusual in the sense that very few people actually take a position and that no doubt I wouldn't be thanked for it. And you know, it was nice reading the letter and telling the story now from the point of view that I won the case, but it took a lot out of me. I mean if I'd lost, I might as well have left.

I find that there are quite a lot of people who mouth about multiculturalism but they're not willing to take up issues. This is a major problem within the schools, not just in Brent. There's still very much an ethnocentric approach. At best, people are just adding things on instead of viewing cultures as of equal value. You have a mainstream curriculum on to which are added options and the pupils can see that if something isn't considered good enough to be placed in the mainstream, it hasn't become 'real knowledge' yet. In my early teaching days, I totally neglected the Irish dimension. I was very into the Afro-Caribbean aspect and getting suitable materials for use in the class-room, but now I'm much more conscious of putting an Irish element into the syllabus. I'm much more active in that respect now.

A few years ago I started teaching a basic Irish class in a community school in Brent and also O and A level classes in Camden. The students who come to those have Irish anyway, some of them are very well read, certainly in Irish literature, but it's a love of the language they have. At the moment I haven't got time to be teaching in Irish, I shouldn't be working in the evenings at all, but I teach Irish now because I feel that time is running out. If classes do not continue at advanced level – and they don't have to be examination classes – the language could die out in London. And if the language dies out, then one hasn't got access to the whole literature that is available in Irish, and that is something that makes me very sad.

Notes

1. Irish speaking area.
2. Accent.
3. 'Can I go out [to the toilet] please, sir?'
4. School inspector.

Recruited from Cork, 1945

When I go back to Ireland, I think those hills belong to me ...

Noreen Hill left Cork for wartime England and settled there. She describes the pressures on women of living in another culture.

I was born in 1922 at 13 Chapel Street, Cork, between the Shandon Bells and the North Cathedral, and that's where I grew up. That's where we all grew up, until we left home. I had three brothers and four sisters. I was the oldest in the family, so everything came back to me for good example.

I always looked on Cork as a beautiful city and I think my father did, and mother as well. I used to talk to my grand-aunts and they told me all about the Troubles, when the Black and Tans were there. The main street in Cork, Patrick Street, was burned down during the Troubles and I heard all about that from my parents.

My father had a good job, he was an engine driver. And although we lived in a very small house, my grandfather and grandmother also lived with us. Downstairs we used to have what you call settee beds, and my brothers slept downstairs and we slept upstairs. We were overcrowded as we grew up, though when my grandparents died it was a bit better then. But my mother wouldn't move from there because we were all born there. And although my father got the chance of living in big houses down the country and places like that, being an engine driver, no way would my mother budge. 'I'm staying here,' she said, 'This is where all my family was born, and I'm staying here.' And to our dismay she would never move. She loved Chapel Street.

My grandmother used to do the housework and my mother used to help her. I was ten when she died – my grandmother. One of my brothers was born the same day. My mother said, 'Your grandma's going out the window and your brother's coming in the door.'

We went to school at the Presentation Convent. It was good, I liked it. I even visited the nuns after getting married and being over in this country. We had to buy our own books, pay for our own ink, buy our own pens – buy everything actually. We had to do all our subjects in both languages, English and Irish, and we had to pass them both. I could speak Irish. When I came over to this country first I was able to speak it very well. Because my grandmother couldn't speak any English, we used to talk it at home. I got the primary certificate but when you got to the intermediate you had to start paying a fee. I went to the intermediate class, but I had to leave because my parents couldn't afford to pay the fee which was quite a lot. I was sixteen then.

When I left school I tried everywhere to get work – bar factories – I didn't want to work in a factory. I wanted to work as a clerk, or I wanted to work inside a shop, a dress shop or something like that. But for that kind of a job they wanted a fee and my father put his foot down. He said he wouldn't pay a fee. 'I fought for this country and I'm not paying a fee for you to go to work – stay at home and help your mother.'

I went to help my aunts – my father's father's sisters – they were top dressmakers in the city. They made for what you'd call at that time the élite, you know, and they charged high prices. So I ran errands for them. In return, they didn't pay me, they'd make a dress or a coat for me. So I usually had a new dress every week, or something like that, because clothes were expensive.

When I was sixteen I hadn't even used make-up. I think I started when I went to my first dance at the convent. I was seventeen then and my aunts made the dress. I enjoyed that – but that was dancing with the nuns! There were no boys at all. And we knew nothing at all about sex – biology wasn't taught by the nuns. My parents never broached the subject. We discussed it at school between us, you know, when a girl'd have her period. She'd think it would be something great and, you know, it would be whispering around the class and that, and giggling. That's how we found out one part of it. But when I came out to this country I knew nothing whatsoever about sex. I was naive, actually. We kind of took it for granted that it was like that. If you were intelligent enough to understand, you'd understand your parents and that they were embarrassed to talk about that sort of thing. All I'd ever heard about girls having babies before they were married, as we put it in those days, was when they were put into the place called The Good Shepherd Convent, and they were left there until somebody claimed them out. And this is what you were threatened with if you weren't home at night at ten o'clock.

I remember when my sister was born, I was twelve I think, and my father put my mother into a private nursing home – because in those days you paid through your wages for this sort of thing. One day I went up to visit her when I came home from school, in my gym frock, you know, and my white blouse.

She was delighted and I was able to give her all the news. My father found out about it and I got a walloping, because I'd been to visit my mother in the maternity home! He never explained. I didn't know what to think, I was mesmerised.

I think it would have been better if things had been more open. I think in those days if parents sat down and talked to their children like they do now and, you know, became friends with them or pals, like you do – like I do with my children – I think it would have been a lot better. But you were on a different planet altogether – they put you there somehow. I used to tell everything to my grandfather. I couldn't communicate with my own father, although I was very proud of him. Especially later in life, when I understood what he'd done for his country, but I could never communicate with him. I could never sit down and talk to him, you know. I could with my mother.

I never thought about politics then, you don't when you're young, but as I grew older I did, these last few years really . . . I had to come to this country to understand about Ireland, and to understand what politics was, and what my father had done. I don't think his family was republican, but in those days, after the Black and Tans, a lot of the young men joined the IRA and the Fianna Scouts.[1] Then, in 1916, my father was one of the men involved in the Rising. He went up to the Post Office in Dublin, from Cork. He was up there with them and I've got photographs there of him. When I was growing up I was very enthusiastic about the elections, and when De Valera[2] would come into Cork I'd be there to meet him. But elections in Ireland in those days were like the ones in America now, you know, there were flags and loudspeakers everywhere. It was great.

I remember the day the Second World War started. After that, things became bad in Cork. We were rationed, and my father was moved from Cork because there wasn't enough coal to run the trains. He was moved to another town and things were tough, you know, at home. My mother was finding it hard to cope, to manage. Then the posters went up, at the Labour Exchange – 'JOIN THE WRENS', 'JOIN THE ATS', 'PLENTY OF WORK IN ENGLAND', 'COME TO ENGLAND AND SEE THE WORLD' – all that sort of thing. So my sister joined the ATS – most of my friends left for England, the ones I went to school with. I was interested in joining the WRENS, so I filled the papers up, and I passed the exams and that, but I failed their medical – so that was it. We couldn't tell my father, he'd blow his top. My mother knew, she didn't mind my sister going away, but she was a bit attached to me. We were very close, and I had a weak chest, you know. She worried a lot about me. I took ill then and went into hospital. While I was there, papers came through to come to England and work with munitions. So, I went.

I didn't think it strange at that time, but I did afterwards when I thought about it, that the Irish government allowed all those posters to come out, although we were neutral. They allowed us to emigrate – there was thousands there was, emigrating from all over Ireland, because there was nothing there for us at all. We couldn't find any work, unless you went to scivvy, scrub floors or something like that, you know. That's the only kind of work, and that was very poorly paid. But no way would I do that, I was always very proud, you know, and I wouldn't go down on my knees for anybody.

Do I remember the journey over? Do I heck! It was one of those old cattle boats, you know, where the cattle were underneath and the passengers on top – you could hear the cattle as you travelled on top. And there was, I think, about five of us from Cork, all the rest were Dublin, Limerick ... Oh, I felt terribly strange.

We arrived anyway in Leicester, and I broke away somehow from the rest of the girls – I'm a terrible rebel – I never stick to rules and regulations and I broke away. I found myself right outside that station you came in today, standing in the middle of the road with two suitcases. I had an address that they gave us at the Labour Exchange but what I wanted to do was to make my own way. I intended to take a taxi, but I didn't know where to get one. And anyway, nobody understood what I was saying, you know. I mean, even when I told the policeman where I was going, he didn't know what I was on about. He asked me to show him the address and he brought me to my first lodgings in Leicester – that was out in Aylestone Road. Oh, it was terrible! I'll never forget it.

Homesick! I couldn't believe that homesickness would kill you, because that's how I felt – that I was dying. I couldn't eat the food because everything was smothered with gravy and, of course, there was powdered eggs, you know, in those days. And I was always fussy about my food. I missed my mother, and I suppose I missed everything really. I felt so bad that I think I could have laid down and died. I felt so homesick, and I think I was like that for about three months. And then I took ill. The doctor wanted to send me back home, and I begged him not to. I didn't want to, I was very independent, and I didn't want to give up, you know, I didn't want to go back and have them say, 'I told you so.' I wanted to soldier on. I had asthma. I always suffered from asthma and I got it very bad. I went to work in an aircraft factory and I think it was, you know, from working nights in the factory. We started work at six at night and we finished at six the following morning – all night long. A week of nights and a week of days, like that, alternately. Five nights, then we had the weekend off. I think we earned £10 if we were lucky, for all that. And I'd always halve that and send some home to my mother. The minute I'd get my wage packet I'd put the money into an envelope and send it to my mother. And then I felt better. Although she wasn't desperate, my father was working and all that, I had other brothers and sisters at home and one of my sisters was very ill at the time and my mother had to pay all the fees for the doctors. And I felt that I was actually with my mother when I sent the money.

Here in Leicester there was rationing, and black-outs. We were able to move freely, but when you changed your address you had to report to the

Noreen Hill

police. You were alien, because our country was neutral and we were under suspicion actually, we were aliens in a country that was at war with Germany. In the police station there was two sides – Alien Visitors, Residents. So we had to go in the Alien door. And if you changed your job or changed your address, you had to report to the police straight away.

When I came over here first, I got a letter from my parish priest, to get the job. You had to have a reference, and not having worked before, I had to get a letter from the priest. The Legion of Mary used to check up on me once a month, from the Church. They'd come to the lodgings and ask the landlady if I went to Mass, and all that. I don't think that happened to everybody.

The first person I met was this Killarney girl and we became very good friends. Her husband played in a band, and the three of us went out together and she used to take me to where her husband played – an Irish club. That was the first social life I had.

Of course, when the war ended we were made redundant. There were a lot of English girls worked there and they were able to go back to hosiery, they had trades like, you know, overlockers. I had no trade, so I was sent to the post office and I got a job delivering letters. It lasted a week. First I was in an area that I knew, but then they sent me to another area. It was a hot summer's day and I couldn't find any of the houses, so I emptied my bag into the box – the post box! And they were most of them registered letters, you know. In those days the lads in the forces were sending their mothers money and that. When I came home, I was really done in. So I went to work the next morning and there were a few chaps there that didn't go in the war and they all looked at me – 'Hey, paddy, you're wanted in the office.' Of course I had to go up to the head postman and he says, 'Sit down.' I sat down. 'Do you realise,' he said, 'that we've had phone calls all night? What did you do that for?' I says, 'I was tired, sir, I couldn't find any of the houses, sir.' 'You told me you knew Leicester.' 'I thought I knew Leicester, sir.' Anyway, he says, 'I'll put you downstairs sorting – you'll be all right sorting.' So he sent me downstairs sorting and I was all right there.

So then we were made redundant there, because the postmen were coming back and they wanted their jobs. So I had to go to the Employment Office again. So he says, 'Can you work a till?' I says, 'No, sir' – it was all 'No, sir' and I was nearly crying. So he says, 'Take this letter to the manageress of the buffet down the London Road station.' I got the job and she taught me how to use the till and of course with the trains passing to and fro it reminded me of my father and brought back a kind of affinity towards the railway, you know, because my father was an engine driver.

When I first came here the language was very difficult too. I remember when I got married my mother-in-law sent me into the Leicester market for some swedes. We didn't call them that in Ireland, we called them turnips. Of course I came back with bananas! Yeah – I didn't know what she was on about. And you feel so stupid. They think you're stupid, because the Irish

96

have that name, although you didn't know at the time what their opinion of the Irish was. You have to be in this country a long while before that comes to you, before the penny drops and you realise what the opinions of lots of people in this country are.

But I intended going back to Ireland. I didn't intend to stay here at all. I was fully intending to go back when the war was over and things got better in Ireland, and hoped I'd find a job. A lot of Irish people are like that. But I got married.

I think I was a year working on the railway when I met Albert. He'd just been demobbed from the Navy. We were going out together for about three months when he asked me to marry him. We met in the January and married in the August. I thought it was great to marry an Englishman! He was quite handsome in those days. My father was very much against it. He wrote a couple of letters to Albert, you know, lecturing him about what marriage was, it's a lifetime job and all that. He wrote then, and said that we should go home before we were engaged. I knew if I brought Albert home before we were engaged that that would be it. I'd be kept home. I was afraid that me father'd throw him out, you know. So I went ahead and married him. We talked it out about Albert being a protestant before I became engaged, and we parted for a while because he wouldn't listen. Then he sent for me and he said he'd do anything I wanted and he said, 'I'll become a catholic when the first child is born.'

The Catholic Church's attitude towards a mixed marriage was very strict. The other person had to go for instruction and had to sign papers that the children would be brought up as catholics. My husband didn't seem to mind that at all — he signed the papers. He didn't discuss it with me, he had a mind of his own about it. If they didn't sign the papers you wouldn't get a dispensation to marry a non-catholic and, of course, they were very much against it in Ireland, the neighbours and everybody. For an Irish person to marry a non-catholic, it was a crime. At the wedding we had the service, but no Mass, like they do now, like you would if you were marrying a catholic.

When I got married first, I had to go and live with my in-laws for a while. Their attitude towards me was hostile. And it was strange, I wasn't long in this country and I didn't understand anything at all about English people. His mother was a very, very good woman, but possessive about Albert especially. He was her older son. And I don't think she thought I was good enough for him, being Irish. Not any other way, but just being Irish, because Irish people had a bad name in this country at that time, because of the IRA putting bombs in pillar boxes, and we were desecrated sort of by that, all Irish people at that time. We didn't get on at all. I felt like a bull in a china shop. I ran home and Albert had to bring me back.

When I first got married, more than anything in the world I wanted a child of my own, but nothing happened for about four years. In the meantime, my sister who was in the ATS got into trouble, and had a baby from an

Englishman. I took my sister home to my mother, and she wouldn't let her come back to this country any more. We told my mother, but not my father, he knew nothing at all about it. My mother was terribly broken-hearted. In those days it was considered a crime, as you know. It was difficult for my sister, but she was frightened I think. My mother told me to go back and take the child out of a home and bring it up. I didn't want to do it but I had to do it for my mother, you know, and for my sister as well. I couldn't leave a little baby in a home. I visited him every Sunday and the more I used to visit, the more I took to him, and of course, I had to obey my mother's wish. She couldn't take the baby. She regretted it after, but she couldn't have the baby in Ireland because of the neighbours. And it would stop my sister from meeting anybody else you know. Her only solution was for me, who was married, to take the baby out and bring it up. It was hard, I know, very hard. Albert was good as well. He did it too.

I was four years being told I couldn't have any children, that my fallopian tubes were blocked. I was broken-hearted. But then I had my fallopian tubes blown by Dr Kearns and he said, 'Go home now and come back when you're pregnant', and I did. And to me that was a miracle. I thought, you know, prayer done it. So, I remember when Albert was born, the whole hospital came to have a look at him, because I had such a job, you know. I had him by Caesarean. I didn't know what labour pains were. I had never heard about labour pains. My mother never discussed these things, they were never discussed. There was no classes in those days, there was no instructions or anything like that. You just went for check-ups. There were no clinics like there are nowadays. The pain was much worse than I expected, afterwards more so, because I was stitched up, you see. But I didn't go into labour with Albert. I went into labour with Michael, because that one was supposed to be a normal birth. But with my asthma, I had an attack of asthma, and I had to have a Caesarean. No such thing as husbands going into the labour, oh no, no, no. The husband tried to keep as far away as possible. He'd be lucky if he was let see the baby straight after it was born! It's only recently that's come into being, isn't it, where the husband can be at the birth? And then it's not all husbands want to. And the way I was brought up I don't think I would have liked him to either.

There's one thing I forgot to tell you, about how innocent I was when I brought Albert home, the very first time, before I had any children. Albert bought a book, it was called *Married Love* – he wanted to show me how to go on – this is a bit personal, now, but it's funny. And Albert put it on the dressing-table upstairs in the bedroom. So one night we were going to bed and he says, 'What are you doing, where's my book?' You see, he couldn't find it, so I said, 'I'll go and ask Mammy if she's seen it.' So I went downstairs to my mother and I said, 'Have you seen Albert's book?' 'What book are you talking about?' she said, 'Is it that book on married love? I've thrown it in the fire. Terrible book,' she says, 'Disgrace.' Albert and me laughed. But of course

98

Albert was ashamed – he was ashamed to come downstairs to face my mother after that. And she was a bit cool with him.

But really, that's how it was. I was very naive. Do you know, it's only in latter years that I knew what a lesbian was. I didn't know what a gay was. I think I found most of my knowledge out by reading. This is how you're brought up, you see, you can't help those things. We're in a permissive age now, and sometimes you're shocked, you know. You get used to it, I mean, if you're a broad-minded person, which I am in a way. But it's the way we were brought up.

I was lucky, in a way, I couldn't have any more children. Some people like big families, but I think for a woman to have eight or nine children, it's a terrible drag on her, bringing children into this world to try to educate them. Can you give them their rights, and can you bring them up the way you want to? It's hard work bringing a large family up. I'm speaking from experience, my mother's experience, and it was harder in those days. There was no children's allowance even. I think contraception is wonderful for women who don't want to have a big family. If it's used properly, I think it's very essential. The Church's attitude towards contraception is a bit biased still, I think. They don't discuss it. I've never heard the priest get up in the pulpit and talk about contraception, in a kind of straightforward way, you know. But abortion, they have talked about that. I think that the Church's attitude towards contraception is wrong. But the majority of Irish families now have two or three children, they keep to the three anyway. I don't think they follow the Church's doctrine any more, like they used to. I think in Ireland – what I found when I was over there this year – they've become very modernised in their ideas now, and Americanised mostly in their outlook. I think a lot of the Irish women over there use contraception, in spite of the Church's teaching, from what I heard.

When I was bringing up my children it was very important to me to try and pass on a sense of Irishness to them. I told them about Irish history, read Irish story books to them, tried to teach them a little bit of the Irish language, tried to teach them their prayers in Irish. I tried to tell them about the Famine, and things like that. But they were very young and I was the only one that could tell them, there was nobody else. No grandmother, no grandfather ... It was very difficult, 'cause there was no place in Leicester you could take the children to in those days where there was any Irish activity, apart from the Church. Their father was British and their grandparents were British and their Irish grandparents were across the Irish sea. They only saw them once a year. We went home every year and they loved it over there.

They were fine while they were in the catholic school. After that, the Irishness dwindled away, apart from what I was trying to inject into them. What they were taught at school I don't know. I don't think the catholic schools in this country teach them much history at all. It's only recently they're trying to bring out history.They know everything about English history, but Irish history is almost nil in the catholic schools, and I think it still is so today. I think the catholic schools here should endeavour to teach at least some Irish history. And I think they should have Irish study classes in the schools as well.

Then, of course, I was married to an Englishman. It's more difficult for an Irish woman who married into an English family, to try to bring her children up good catholics and teach them Irishness, than it would be for two Irish people marrying in this country. All the responsibility of Irishness is on you. I did as much as I could, and as much as I had time to do. They understand Ireland, of course. It's everywhere around here. I've got the flag up there and I've got my father's photograph, in 1916. When they come here, for tea and that, it's all religion and Irishness. To me, everything begins with history, history is the beginning and the end of an Irish person. And that is how I can portray it to them. I can't talk about it, but I can put it here, so that they'll remember it. There's a lot of families like that in this country. It's very sad.

What I regret is that there was no Irish centre in Leicester. If we had a centre, the young people growing up could take their children there, and they'd meet other Irish children. I did write a journalistic story all about this once – about bringing children up in this country, where the mother is Irish and they've got a kind of schizophrenic personality. They're half Irish, and they're half English.

When the Northern Ireland troubles first started I used to sit here, and Michael, my son, would sit there on the settee and the television would come on. And, of course, as you know, the minute the television was turned on, the first thing was Northern Ireland. They revelled in it – you had it for breakfast, dinner and tea. When I'd sit here and see the soldiers with their guns at the street corner, although I come from Southern Ireland I'd say, 'Look at him. Look at them. Look at the bastards, they shouldn't be there.' And I'd start ranting and raving, you know – at the television, not at my son. The next thing, my husband would say, 'Turn off the television.' And my son would say, 'They're murderers.' I'd say, 'They're not murderers, you're Irish too.' 'I'm not Irish, I'm English.' So in the end, I'd go out of the living room, go upstairs, and leave the room to my husband and son. Because my husband was on my son's side, I was on my own.

My children describe themselves as being English. This is their country. Although young Albert said that sometimes when the bombs were dropped, you know, and people said 'Those paddies are at it again', and they'd start criticising, and he said, 'I always stick up for the Irish, mother.' They're men now. They're living a different life. You only know them as children, you don't know them as men, I think.

In some ways it's maybe easier to assimilate to English ways, if you're that way inclined. If you put your Irishness behind you. There are friends of mine, Irish girls, who don't mix with the Irish people at all, except an odd dance now and again, you know, and who don't be bothered with their own Irish people. I think a lot of Irish people are frightened. I think that they keep to themselves, you know, they don't say much, only among themselves. They're scared of public opinion. They seem frightened of expressing themselves, you know. When there's an Irish do on at the local church hall, and all the Irish people are there – at the end it's 'Faith of our Fathers'.[3] They used to play 'The Soldier's Song',[4] but now it's 'Faith of our Fathers'! I get into arguments about my Irishness. I wear an Easter Lily, I go down to Mass, I don't care, it's me, that's what I feel. They wouldn't wear an Easter Lily for fear they'd be counted as IRA supporters, or something like that.

We integrate, you know. Some Irish people – you can't even tell when they speak that they're Irish. They lose their dialect and everything. You can't tell them apart. Whereas other ethnic groups, like the Asians, they're different. The way I look at it, I get on the bus, or I'm in the shop, or in the post office and I can hear those people talking away in their own language. God, they're lucky! They've got a real identity; not only the colour of their skin, but they've got their language as well. You can't blame the Irish people, the ordinary Irish person for the loss of their language. You've got to blame this country. They did away with it. They rubbed it out, as well as trying to rub the culture out. We've got to keep the culture alive.

When I first started writing to *The Irish Post*, I had lost all my confidence, because I had an accident. I wasn't badly injured, but it took all my confidence, then I started writing. When I wrote to the *Post* it was about two lines – 'Why doesn't someone take that Mr Paisley by the hand and teach him the facts of life?' And then I decided to go in for the short story competition. The family were making fun of me, ' 'Twill end up in the dustbin, Mam.' I still wrote it though. It was called 'The Girl from Cork' and was based on my own life. I couldn't believe it when I was commended. I think that gave me confidence. They said, 'Keep on writing.' So I went to the creative school of writing at the adult education, and I learned a few things there.

I don't think there's anything been written at all about Irish women. I suppose nobody ever bothered about them. Well, in Ireland, women are ignored, aren't they? If you look back, when my mother was growing up, we were not allowed into a pub. If we did, we had to go into a side bar, a little snug they called it, and we weren't allowed to mix with the men. Even when I got married, my father thought it was awful if I went out to a pub with my husband. We are ignored, yes, and I think it's the same here. Women are ignored, Irish women especially, because they keep in the background, leave the men doing the talking. I mean, in Ireland, my mother had to clean my father's shoes, have them there ready for him, and all his clothes on a Sunday morning, and that sort of thing. When you became a wife, you became a slave as well. That's how I looked at it, when I was growing up. I was very kind of observant when I was growing up, because I remember on one occasion – when my mother was in hospital – my father said, 'Clean them shoes'; I wouldn't clean them. 'No, no fear,' I says, 'I'm not cleaning your shoes. I will never clean any man's shoes.' And that's what I was, a bit of a rebel. I think that Irish women have been pushed into the background. I think it's time they were brought into the limelight, don't you?

I've been in this country now over forty years, and as a matter of fact, I'm more politically-minded now, and my identity is stronger than ever it was. More so than when I came first. I think that was because I married into a British family. I mean, I remember the first time I was taking my husband over to Ireland, his mother said, 'He won't be shot when he arrives, will he Noreen? They won't shoot him because he's an Englishman?' This is the ignorance. So, I said, 'Oh, no, we're not savages over there you know. We're quite normal.' I remember that, that is the truth. I mean, you can't blame her in a way, but she thought when her son would arrive in Ireland, he'd be shot. This is how it was, you see, this is the way things were.

I'm proud of my identity, I'm proud of being Irish. I love Ireland, although I never got anything there. It never done anything for me. But it's the country. When I go back to Ireland on holidays I look around me and think, those hills belong to me, and that's my grass, and that's the way I feel. I can't say it, as long as I've been in this country, I can't feel that way, you know. I'll never go back to Ireland, but my spirit is there. That's how I feel about Ireland.

Notes

1. Nationalist Boy Scouts organisation, founded by Countess Markievicz in 1909.
2. One of the commandants of the Irish Volunteers during the 1916 Rising and the only one who wouldn't permit women to serve under his command. He was sentenced to death by the British but was imprisoned instead. He supported anti-Treaty forces in the civil war, but later as leader of the Fianna Fáil party, he accepted de facto reality of partition. He defined women's place as being in the home in the 1937 Constitution, of which he was one of the main architects.
3. A catholic hymn.
4. The Irish National Anthem.

To Scotland from Ulster

'Time flies over us, but leaves its shadow behind'

Margaret Collins describes growing up against a background of divisions between catholic and protestant in the North of Ireland and talks about her life in England, including her involvement in her trade union.

I come from Coalisland in Tyrone, down by Lough Neagh. It's a lovely sort of area. When you're away from it you appreciate how lovely it is. I grew up on a farm, with my four brothers and two sisters – it wasn't a home farm, but about twenty acres of land that my father and mother had bought and we lived further down the road in a rented house. It wasn't a big farm, but there was always three or four cows and calves, and my mother kept hens and pigs so there was always a few ready to go to market. It was by the lake and my father used to fish eel and they were all exported to London.

It was a very catholic area we lived in, only two families were protestants. We were a hundred yards from the school and those children all went away three miles to the protestant school. There was no mixing, not with the country people, or even in the towns. There's a town called Stuartstown that is equally as near as Coalisland, but we never associated ourselves with Stuartstown, that was a protestant town. There were some mixed marriages, but certainly it wouldn't have happened in our house. We did have cousins that were married to protestants but that was really frowned on. When I was about fifteen another girl and I went to join the Red Cross, which was mainly protestant. It was all right while we were at the classes, but socially you didn't mix at all. I can remember once we went to a dance that was run for the Red Cross and her and I just stuck out like sore thumbs. I don't know when we became aware of those divisions ... from a very early age. You just grew up knowing that they'd got all that was going. It didn't worry you.

My mother and father had a terrible time with the Black and Tans and the B-men.[1] They lost their little home through them. The Black and Tans burnt the house down. My father worked as a farm labourer in the Stuartstown area, and the house belonged to the people he worked for. My mother reckoned that they just wanted us out of the area. She'd heard that there'd been trouble in Coalisland that day, and that the Black and Tans were more or less on the rampage. Earlier in the day the little one came in and said she'd found a bathbrick, but it was a round of ammunition and it had been planted. I don't know why, but my mother and father just knew that they would get a visit that night. My mother had three children and was pregnant with Kevin, and she said that my father and her had to leave, take the children out of bed and carry them. As they got up to the top of this hill and rested, they could see the lights of these Crossley Tenders as they called them, coming up towards their house, and they saw the house go up in flames. If they'd stayed there ... After that my mother went home to her own people – where I was born – and stayed. My father got this rented house and they never went back to that area ever any more.

As kids we listened to stories about the Black and Tans – my mother could've told them all day long. You just grew up feeling bitter and anti-'them' – anti-British because it was the Black and Tans, and anti-protestant because the B-men at that time were probably worse. They were doing it to their neighbours and people that they knew, which was worse.

When I was twelve the war broke out, and then things started getting better. Money started getting more plentiful because there was a British aerodrome built down the road from where we lived, and work got very plentiful early in the war. The first time I remember being conscious of the South was when chaps came to work at the aerodrome and they were from Limerick and Tralee and Mayo. I must've been fifteen the first time I went to Dublin. Dublin was like the Mecca. It was the place you went to if you were a republican, you went to the centre, to O'Connell Street. I changed my mind about it as I got older! I was nearly as old the first time I went to Belfast, which was a lot nearer.

I left school when I was fourteen and had a year at home. Then two other girls and myself used to go to this woman in Stuartstown who was a private teacher. She taught us English, maths, a bit of bookkeeping and shorthand and she started doing biology. I went to her for two years. My mother paid for that. The job prospects were very poor. There was a factory but I never was interested. There wasn't that many women that travelled to the towns to work. Young girls just stayed at home, but that wasn't a bad thing because

Opposite: Margaret Collins

that was in the forties and the war was still on, and money was good because the men had plenty of work.

I left Ireland in 1945, a couple of months before I was eighteen. My friend Bridie was a year older than me – Bridie O'Neill who's now dead, may she rest in peace – and she had gone to Scotland. The first time she came home, she asked me to go back with her. The matron in the hospital where she worked asked her to tell any girls that she knew, that wanted to come over, that she would like to have them. I'd never been to the unemployment office, but Bridie had been there and this is where she had been recruited from. They were always looking for girls for London. My mother wouldn't let me go to London but she let me go to Scotland. I went on my own from Belfast to Glasgow and stayed with some friends who'd been over during the war. They met me at the boat in Glasgow and I stayed three or four days with them, and then they put me on the train for Aberdeen. It wasn't too bad when I was with them because there was that connection with home and people I knew, but I do remember how lonely it was when I went to Aberdeen. I just missed my family.

Once I was there a little while and made friends with the girls it was quite like being in Ireland. But, there were only the two of us Irish girls, and that was the first time I knew what it was to be in an argument over religion. It would come up because I used always to go to Mass. It used to be awkward, especially when you had to do night duty and you wanted to go to Communion. You had to fast all night, and then you'd come off duty and you would walk the three miles into the town to go to Mass. Oh yes, there was a couple of them I can remember who were quite anti-catholic, and they were telling me how stupid I was. There was hardly any Irish in that area. I met a few Irish going to Mass, but they were mostly men that had been in the British Airforce, as there was quite a few airfields around there.

I liked nursing. It was the comradeship side of things with the girls . . . it was enjoyable work. You were always told to behave like a lady, they were always comparing what it was to be a nurse to what it was to work in a factory or to work in a shop – you were above that. When I finished my training I came to London and got a job in St Stephen's in Fulham. I met my husband at the Garryowen dance hall. We moved to Hackney in the fifties after we got married and it was very hard to get a flat then – as hard as it is now, it never got any easier. There wasn't many Irish around here at that time, but I never encountered any anti-Irish prejudice then.

I can well remember having my first baby. It was a long labour – I had a pain in my back for two days and a pain in my sides. I phoned my friend and she says, 'Sounds like you've got a kidney infection' – she was a mother of two children! My husband was at work and I remember getting my antenatal card and going up to the hospital. I look back now and feel sorry for myself. There was a woman going into the hospital in front of me, and her husband and sister and mother were all with her, and I was going in with nothing, only my card! The midwife said to me, 'Have you got your ration book with you? And where's your clothes?' I'm trying to tell her it's just these pains y'know, and she said, 'You're in labour', and I wouldn't believe it!

We didn't know what to expect, we were told childbirth wasn't pain, it was discomfort! This woman said to me, 'You know, you could go on like this for three or four days.' I remember thinking I couldn't go on with this for three or four days! I'm sure I told my husband afterwards how painful it was. I wouldn't have missed an opportunity like that! Though I wonder how much some men really grasp about it, even today.

We had four children altogether and they were brought up very conscious that they were Irish. I brought them to Ireland every year, I never missed a year, and we'd go for the whole six weeks. That was no joke – it was such an ordeal – the train journey to Heysham and then all night on the boat to Belfast, with small children and two suitcases! I had to bring summer clothes, winter clothes, wellies, the lot.

I remember one year travelling with the four of them. The eldest was seven and the baby was four months and the train arrived late at the boat so, of course, the boat was packed. We had to go down into the lounge and it was full of men stretched out full on the seats and couches. Nobody moved or took any notice of us and I got angry at this. So I asked if somebody could just sit up to make some room for us but still nobody budged. I got really angry then and another woman with kids came up behind me and backed me up and we both started. Then they moved . . . we'd lots of room then!

When my youngest was at primary school I got a job as a home help. I thought I'll do this for a year or two until he's at secondary school, and it ended up I was there fourteen years! That was when I got involved with NUPE. The council were dishing out shoes and overcoats and nobody could wear the coats and nobody could use the shoes because they didn't fit properly, so I went to the union. From then on I got involved. The woman that'd been a shop steward – she was from Cork – had left, and I just kind of fell in for it. I was getting women to join. I'd say, 'If you don't belong to a union you can't expect the union to fight for you.' So at that time I got quite a few women to join. I'm nursing again now, but I still belong to NUPE. I just stayed with them – anything I need I can always go to NUPE. I belong to the working party of the joint works committee, where the employers meet the employees, and I attend all the branch meetings. There's not many Irish women involved – I don't think Irish women are very conscious of trade unions. But I can understand people not being involved. In our branch women outnumber the men and at branch meetings there's always a few more women than men – but men don't want women. They don't want to hear women's voices at all, they talk women down. That's your own colleagues, in the same branch!

Also, they're really anti-Irish. They don't want to know anything at all about Ireland. There's two people I can talk to about it, but on the whole, they don't want to know. When we had miners from Kent, one of them told about being intimidated by the police, and abused. I just said, 'Well, that's how we've been treated in Northern Ireland, maybe you'll understand now', and one of the miners said, 'That's right, sister.' But it just died at that. I remember it came up at the end of one meeting that there'd be a demonstration in support of Northern Ireland and it was shouted down. Just thrown out. That was quite a big meeting and I was mad. I get very annoyed.

For years I've been trying to explain about Ireland, not just in the union, but with other English people. They all look on you as being a nice person, but they just can't understand how you feel this way. I don't get depressed, I get mad, and then I get in a bad temper and I can't say anything. I could cry then with anger. I just get so angry. Irish jokes really annoy me. At work they might say, 'Will I tell you an Irish joke?' and I'll say, 'No. I don't want to hear any Irish jokes. You can joke about yourselves, you're a bigger laugh than we are.' I never apologise for being Irish. I know some incidents happen that you couldn't condone, but you just have to try to explain to people why it happened, just try to explain the Northern Irish situation. I think the Irish have been their own worst enemies. They've all kept too quiet, probably hoping it'd go away. The older people just want to lead a quiet life and not get involved. I do admire people that'll go out and speak up.

Notes

1. An armed auxiliary police force, overwhelmingly protestant.

Against the Odds

Dear Daughter

'IT SEEMED to me as I was growing up, that women were like an appendage to men, whereas men had a life all of their own and different things could happen in their lives. But a woman and her children were attached to a man and her life depended on what he allowed her to do and on where he went. She never had a life of her own, she virtually never went any place on her own. That's my mother's generation I'm talking about.'

*

'SEX was never mentioned. If you asked your mother, "Where did I come from?" she'd say, "Under a gooseberry bush." The only thing they would say to you when you were going out was, "Don't let anybody touch your clothes." Your mother would say that and you had the impression that somebody came and stole your clothes, ran away with them. So, it was more frightening because children sense things even if adults don't talk about them. You knew when you started going out with boys that there was something, but you didn't know what it was.'

*

'I'VE A CLEAR recollection of when I first had my period. I was only eleven at the time. My mother said, "Now that this has happened to you, you must never go near boys while you're bleeding like this. Keep away from them, because now you're becoming a woman." But she never gave me any explanation. Anything I found out was by talking to other girls. There was a lot of sniggering, and I really hated it. In fact, I didn't talk to them about it because I didn't like the behind the doors attitude, you know. I don't think I had any reservations about my body. As a girl, I could feel a pleasure in my body – that I was developing and things. I think I totally accepted that I was female, and that I would inevitably get married and have children. It didn't seem at all unattractive, it just seemed inevitable somehow, and something that would prevent me exploring a whole lot of other things. I suppose I totally accepted that with one part of me, although I was independent and exploring all sorts of ideas with another side of myself.'

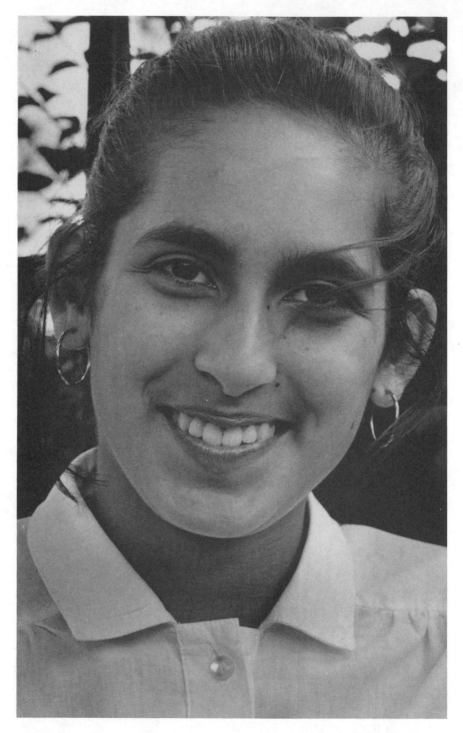

Carrying the can

Irish Constitution

Article 41 2.2   The State shall, therefore, endeavour to ensure that mothers shall not be obliged by economic necessity to engage in labour to the neglect of their duties in the home.

'KILKENNY was a very happy, friendly place. I really can never remember it raining, only sunny. Everyone knew everyone else, so there was always someone to visit. In the early years my mother left us with my grandmother and came to England and worked in factories for months at a time. My father never really lived with us, he was away in the British Army for a while, but really he just wasn't responsible.

In 1947 he said that they were going to get a home together in England and asked my mother to come across with us. We came Rosslare/Fishguard and a long train journey to Paddington Station, and he wasn't even there to meet us. He said he'd be there, that he'd got a flat and this, that and the other; but he'd let her down. I can remember sitting on the cases, I might have been five or six, while my mother went making phone calls and rushing round trying to get somewhere to stay. My auntie put us up for the night. There were four of us – five, four, three and one – babes in arms.

Then my mother got a flat through a friend she'd worked with, and went to the army benevolent fund, or somewhere, and they gave her camp beds. I can remember vividly having breakfast off an orange box, turned on its side, and I think at that point she got a cleaning job, and the smaller children were put in a nursery. She may have gone to my father's mother, who lived near, for help, because she always supported my mother. Her husband had acted in the same way towards her, and I think she felt my father should be more responsible.

My father turned up two weeks later, in a drunken state, but my mother was so forgiving, she would always take him back and this went on for years. I suppose she thought it would be wrong to break the marriage up, that it hadn't really had a chance, that they'd never had a home of their own. Every move she made was towards that end. But it just didn't work out because it got to the stage where other women were involved. One day, a young lady, pregnant, arrived at the door and he was the father of that baby. My mother was there, also pregnant with her fifth child. So that was the start of the real separation and trouble between them.

I mean, he was still like a single chap – he might as well have never married. He absolved himself of all responsibility and left everything to my mother. I thought it was unfair, that he would arrive when he had a good win on the dogs or horses and he'd bring great big dolls. If it was somebody's birthday – if he remembered – he'd bring a great big cake and everything in the garden was going to be lovely. It might last two weeks and then he'd be gone. Just out of the blue, he'd go out to buy a packet of cigarettes and he wouldn't come back.

I can really remember upsetting him once. One night he came back. It was soon after this young lady being round, and I think my mother must have mentioned something about getting separated, or she didn't think it was going to work, and he got violent and actually threw her down the stairs. She was about six or seven months pregnant at the time, and he threw the milk bottles after her, from outside the kitchen door. I remember getting out of bed, coming to the top of the stairs and he was there with his back to me. I jumped on him and I hit him. I said, 'Leave my mother alone' or something, 'She's the only one who's good to us and you ought to be ashamed of yourself' and all the rest of it, and I remember him sitting down and actually crying on the stairs. He just sat there crying, saying he didn't mean it and all the rest of it, and things were going to be wonderful. But it just didn't work.

I think that sometimes my mother may have thought that she didn't know where to turn or what would happen next. But she's a coper; she copes. The new baby was put straight into the nursery with the other little ones and my mother got a job in the dry cleaning shop, ironing all day, just two doors away from where we lived where she could keep an eye on us and at the same time she might be able to pop in and make us some tea after school.

She was always trying to keep things together and in the end, when things got too much, she would send us to Ireland and try and work. If she'd gone back to Ireland, she'd have had no money at all from any source. My grandmother would always take us and look after us and obviously my mother wasn't paying the fares. That continued until I was fourteen, and I went to school in both places. When my grandmother died, it was my Auntie Maura, she'd moved into my grandmother's house to look after their unmarried brother. She had five children of her own and her husband had gone to work in England and never came back. But he was sending her money and maintaining her, and we'd go and stay there.

It's funny though, when it came to the point where my mother wanted to separate and start fresh, the family were against that. Well, the catholic idea of divorce – it was wrong. They thought she should really just stay in Ireland and bring us up. But I don't think she had any choice about getting a divorce. She was in the situation that if life was going to get better for anyone, herself included, it was the only way she could do it. But when she finally divorced, I think it was a relief to her family. My grandmother was dead, and the others thought it was the best thing all round. I'm glad she did. She met my stepfather and it worked out. I see him as my father really.

If it hadn't been for her my life would have been very different, so with all of us. We'd have been in a home somewhere, being cared for. She was very brave really, to keep us all together. I don't think it was a very difficult start for me, not really. I think you learn a lot from it, that you've got to be independent and, you know, cope.'

Women and children at the Roundwood Irish festival

A timeless, timeless thing

'THE ONLY nice thing I remember about being in labour was when one of the midwives came up to me, held my hand and I remember her saying my name. And it was a tremendous feeling. Going through that made me realise the closeness of birth and death in a sense. It makes me aware of how much people who are dying in hospital do need someone to hold their hand, just to say their name. There are tremendous parallels with women in childbirth. Yet many people are just left alone.'

*

'I REMEMBER coming down the stairs and there was a very young girl and her husband going up to the labour ward, and the girl said to me "How is it up there?" "Oh," I said, "it's great . . . once you get to the top." And I looked up after her and I thought, "May God help you." You just don't know what's before you, and no woman does.'

*

'I WOKE up at five o'clock and it was June. It was a lovely hospital set in its own grounds and the impression I have is of this warm sunny morning and the birds just singing everywhere around and this glorious feeling that it was all over. I think it was the greatest high I've ever had.'

The tender trap

'I GOT married after I'd been over here for a year. I didn't want children, I knew that and children and marriage were interwoven as it were, but I wanted to be with Eddie, so it was the tender trap I suppose. In our circle people didn't just live together, getting married was the only way really.'

*

'AFTER Liam had gone for two years, I went to get a legal separation, and the solicitor said to me "I think you're wasting your time, get a divorce. He's been gone a long time now." In my own mind I wondered if I should or shouldn't. The Catholic Church is against divorce. My own catholic background had helped me a lot and I'd always kept my religion up. But from the point of view of getting my life sorted out – he wasn't any good to me or the kids, he'd never provided a penny any of the times he'd been gone and I didn't want to go on getting legal separations and taking him back again. At the same time, from the catholic point of view, I felt by getting a divorce I was the one to blame. I still felt punished when I met my second husband and we decided to get married, and I couldn't get married in a Catholic Church. I felt very bad then. He was being punished for something he couldn't help, and his family – to them he was just marrying a divorced woman, and they've never really forgiven me for that.

I think myself the Church could make it a bit easier for people who've been badly treated for a number of years. I was told I could've got my marriage annulled, but it would take a long, long time and a lot of money and questions. Getting divorced I could go to church all right, but I could never receive the sacraments. Then my second husband died and they tell me I can go to Communion now, because as far as they're concerned I'm still married to the first. So I refuse to go. I feel that badly, but I refuse to go because I feel that they punished my second husband and now, because he's dead, it makes everything all right for me.'

For better or worse

'WHEN I became pregnant I didn't know what to tell my mother, how to cope with it. I was upset, and excited – it's a funny kind of mixture. I was pregnant and I was only seventeen. I went to a local doctor, who a friend recommended to me. He was, and continued to be through my three years of marriage, one of the most supportive people I've ever met. I couldn't speak highly enough of him, because he was unique. He confirmed that I was pregnant. He said "What do you want to do? Have a good think about it. Do you want me to help you to tell your parents?" You know, a lot different from what other doctors in the area would be.

I couldn't face it. In the end, because I had all this building up inside, I just walked out of the house and just didn't come back. I went to stay with a friend, just went missing from home completely. Nobody knew where I was. Eventually, my mother tracked me down after three days. My friend told her, and my mother just cried. That was awful. She told my father, and he was fine. It was a big relief to get it off my shoulders. We discussed what was going to happen. My mother said "You have the baby, stay at home and you can go back to school. Don't marry him, please." A tentative suggestion was an abortion. "Nobody need know about it." But I decided I was going to get married. We argued and fought about that but I was quite convinced from the start that that was what I wanted to do. I got married in a little church in Galway.

The baby was due in January, but she wasn't born until 27 February. It was a long labour, it continued all night until ten past one in the day. In all that time my husband hadn't even rung the hospital. I was in hospital, I think, for about six or seven days, and he didn't come very much. I think I realised after I married him that I'd made a big mistake. Things had started to go wrong – he had started to drink, and wasn't coming home. In the first month I was married I knew that I was slowly planning my getaway, from there on in. I knew that eventually, sooner rather than later, I would leave. I knew that there was no way I was going to end up forty years later a broken person, living with an animal like this. Absolutely no way.

Anyway, I came home with the baby and that was a bit frightening. I wanted to go home to my mother for a week, and she wanted me to come, but he wouldn't allow me to go. Things started to get worse. I couldn't talk to anybody. I got to the stage where he would come home from work and say "What have you done today?", and I would have to give a complete rundown of who I spoke to, who I met, what I'd done. If I was offered a lift from the town — we lived about a quarter of a mile from the town — I had to refuse!

Then, the actual beating started. I mean I was really badly beaten, black eyes, everything. I was left unconscious on the floor. My hair was pulled out. I couldn't leave my head on a pillow, the pain was so bad. In the morning he realised what he'd done, because I just looked a wreck. My eyes were black, my mouth was all cut inside. He went next door and said that I'd fallen down the stairs, and could they get a doctor. He'd got to go to work.

The doctor knew immediately. He said "Did he do this to you?" I denied it. I rang my husband's brother and he took me into hospital. He knew, but he never asked what happened. He never asked. I mean, the journey took half an hour, and all during that time we never talked about my face, and I looked a wreck. In the hospital I met a nurse who knew me, and I thought "Oh, she knows." The doctors asked me how it happened, and I still kept lying. That was the first major instance, and it just continued onwards and onwards and it carried on for three years.

I couldn't tell anybody, because every evening I was threatened, "You can't tell anybody, otherwise I'll finish you off for good." I was still seventeen, and I had young friends, and if you walk around and you have a black eye and you've got marks — my neck used sometimes be marked — people *do* suspect and people talk in small towns, and they knew. I couldn't tell my parents. I was afraid, it was absolute fear. I felt nobody would support me. My sister was one of the first people that actually found out about it, and she said "Just don't tell my mother."

The neighbours knew it was happening, and were sometimes frightened for me, they told me afterwards. The few times that I ran next door and got away from him they locked the doors and kept him out. In the end, I really was so terrified of him, I began to lose weight. I couldn't eat at all. I was just a wreck physically. I weighed about six and a half, seven stone. I looked dreadful. I would go to my parents every Sunday and when he would say it was time to go I would just have a funny look on my face. I dreaded going home.

He could be really, really nice to people. People assumed we were very happy because if I went out with him, if I didn't look happy I was told when I got home. We'd go into a pub, and if I didn't say the right thing, he would pinch me, so that people wouldn't see, or twist my arm behind my back and threaten me.

I left him several times. My father said, "I don't think you should go back to him really", but invariably I did. My mother was under pressure because the neighbours were looking, and my sister was still at school and it was, you know, a bit much for them. When I finally left he wouldn't accept it, and he told people for about nine months after I'd left that I was still there. Somebody actually beat him up one night because of what had happened, and he went to the police station to report it, and they said, "Sorry, we don't want to know", because they knew what he'd done to me.

I was the only person in the area that had left a man. People's reactions were quite interesting. You do become – not a figure of fun exactly – but people feel that once you've been married, divorced or separated, that you are available. I was almost raped once because this guy that I've known since I was ten or twelve assumed I was fair game. It was really shocking.

In the end I decided that it was definitely time to leave, to go away, because the pressures were too much. I came to London, because my aunt lived here and I could stay with her temporarily. When I found a flat eventually, it was the greatest joy to be able to come in and close the door at night and not have the worry and sheer terror of waiting for somebody like that to come in.'

Choices

'IT TOOK me years to come out as a lesbian. Looking back on it I think it was always in me; my first attraction towards women came when I was eleven or twelve. Being gay was only mentioned very occasionally, but it was disparaged completely. I mean, it was the pits of sin and sodomy. It was an absolutely awful thing and I internalised that and I felt ashamed about it, and tried to suppress it. I grew up in a rural area in the sixties and seventies. If you were a woman and you didn't get married, you left. I mean there wasn't really any place for you, like there might be in a town, it was all families and married couples. I'm sure I would never have come out unless I left Ireland.

Although I came to London to do other things as well, unconsciously I think being lesbian was one reason I left. Coming here and finding the sort of people that gave support for that brought me out as a lesbian really. I don't know if I would have managed it if feminists and other Irish lesbians hadn't made such an impression on me. There were quite a lot who had been here for a long time before me. The Irish lesbian network was very important, I think it still is.

It still took me quite a long while to come around to admitting to myself that this was my identity. It wasn't really until I had a relationship with a woman that I could. We were friends for quite a number of years and then we began this relationship. I had known her even before I left Ireland, and that was important, that she was another Irish woman and we had a similar understanding coming from the same situation and background. Emotionally I felt I had come home – it was a homecoming.'

'I WAS terrified to be pregnant, and frightened of a termination as well. I felt the pregnancy was an accident. There was a lot of stigma attached to being single and pregnant although it was England and the seventies. At the antenatal clinic everyone was called "Mrs" but single mothers were called by their first names. That's actually why I didn't have a termination, because they were so horrible and because they presumed that you'd come for one. I just reacted. This consultant sat with his back to me and shouted, "I suppose you want to get rid of it." So I just reared up and said "No, of course we don't." A complete double fiction! But I did everything effort would do to miscarry, so it was a plain miracle the baby was born.

There was absolute mayhem when my family heard. They felt I had done this deliberately to upset them, that I was thirsting after new experiences and not thinking about them. I wrote home to them, putting a good face on it, knowing they would have hell to pay at their end and saying, "I'll cope fine. I'll just stay over here and say nothing if you want." That was apparently the wrong thing to do, because for years they have gone on about how hurtful that letter was. There was no support; they were furious and hurt. So I didn't go home, I just kept out of it.

During the labour I had a great midwife and when the baby was born the feeling was instant. As soon as she appeared I adored her and it wiped out everything that had gone before. This doctor said to me, "Well, when are you getting married?" and I shouted "What for? I've no intention of getting married." Once I'd had her I was able to shout at him. I wasn't before. Having her gave me a lot of independence – it was the two of us and them really.'

*

'ABORTION was never, ever talked about. There was just a total silence about it when I was growing up. It was one of those things that some people did when they had to, to get the problem out of the way, but it wasn't the right thing to do and you had to keep quiet about it.

When I decided to have an abortion, it was because I thought it would be much too painful and difficult to have a baby on my own and I wasn't getting on too well in my relationship. I couldn't cope with having a baby then. All kinds of things came up – like not feeling grown up enough to look after somebody else and not feeling able to actually face people at home and say, "All right, this is what I've decided to do. I'm not what you think I am." Y'know, there was the image of the career girl living in London and all that! But also, I'd always said that if I had kids I would get married, partly to fit in with my family and partly because I'm trapped into that idea of security and maybe, I think, that for me it would be some kind of security as well. It didn't really feel like a choice, no, it felt like it was something I had to do. In a way, it was a non-choice. There wasn't any other option.

While I was pregnant, I felt so invaded and out of control which was probably tied up with the fact that I knew I had to have an abortion. But there were elements of it I quite liked too – it made me feel special in some strange kind of way, like something exciting physically was happening, but I couldn't possibly have gone ahead with it.

I had been involved in the campaign for women's abortion rights earlier on, so I knew all about it theoretically. To me it seems absolutely obvious that the woman has more of a right than a foetus, but I hadn't really realised what it was like for women and how much they go through in their minds to get to the point of having an abortion. When I actually had the abortion, I think I'd underestimated how alone I would feel. Because I'd worked it out rationally and it was a great relief that I was sure it was what I wanted, I'd underestimated just how bad I'd feel in the hospital, waiting. Afterwards, I felt relief and really strong at having made that decision, but also a weird sense of loss, like at the end of a relationship or something like that. The pain after the operation was like some kind of punishment – not a punishment for having an abortion, but punishment for having sex and thinking I could be liberated and free! Luckily, I could talk to my sister about it.

I couldn't possibly tell my parents and I suppose the secrecy makes it harder, but I'm not sure . . . I told nearly everybody I'm close to at work and I remember thinking, if this was in Ireland, there's no way you could do that. There is less of a taboo over here, I think, it doesn't seem to be such a desperately secret area. Maybe some day it could be an everyday topic of discussion but I don't know because I don't think it'll ever be an easy thing to do.

When it was all over, I kept waiting for this bombshell to drop, for me to think, "Oh, I've done the wrong thing." And it never ever did. I feel absolutely as sure now as I did then which is comforting.'

*

'SINGLE women are still not really accepted. You're only half a person. In the community at large, if you're a woman on your own, you're not a complete person; there's something a bit wrong with you if you haven't managed to have a male tag along with you. You're definitely at a disadvantage. You don't get asked out because it's awkward to have an extra woman hanging around. She's too fat, or too plain, or too anything you like, it's never accepted that a woman could make a deliberate choice not to get married. They don't accept that. And this is as true of the English community too – it's not just the Irish community. You go to dances and you're always expected to have a partner. You go on holiday, you must have a partner and generally, partner means someone of the other sex. No, there's no realisation that people can opt out of marriage.

I've never been completely tied to anybody, which is what I couldn't bear to be. I don't feel that anyone, man or woman, should feel tied to another person. It's an insult to their individuality. It's an insult to their humanity, to tie two people together. Every individual is a person in his or her own right. They have the right to walk free as themselves.'

Bringing the Children

Too much to ask?

Betty McDowell talks about the conflicts within Irish society which left her, a mother of six children, little option but to leave for England.

I was born in Belfast in 1931, which was the year before the great outdoor relief strike.[1] My father used to tell me that it was the last time that catholic and protestant workers marched down the High Street together. After that, they were systematically broken up. He himself was told that if he joined the Orange Order[2] he would never be out of work, and he did. Practically everyone was unemployed in Belfast in 1931, catholic and protestant. But after that there was systematic discrimination in favour of the protestants, and that's what the whole society was built on, rather than on religious liberties, as some protestants would like to think.

My father wasn't a member of the Labour Party, but my Uncle Joe and Auntie Tillie were. They suffered a lot for it. She was a boxmaker and helped to organise the unions in Belfast. She got a bronze medal for her work. Because of her trade union activity she was sacked from her job and was never able to get a job in Belfast after that. In fact, she came to England and joined the Navy. That was a fairly familiar pattern for anybody who was a socialist, or even active in the labour movement, they had to emigrate. And these were staunch protestants.

I suppose these are my earliest memories. My father and my auntie used to tell me about these things when I was very young. He taught me to sing the 'Red Flag'.[3] In fact, he taught me to sing 'Kevin Barry'[4] as well as 'The Sash My Father Wore'.[5] I suppose I got my republican ideas and my socialist ideas from my father, although he was an Orangeman. He had this knowledge about the Labour Movement and told me about 1798,[6] and whetted my appetite to know about these things. So, on the one hand I was brought up very strictly and staunchly protestant, but on the other hand there was a doorway through which I could go and enquire about the other side.

I didn't learn Irish history at school. It was English history we learnt, of course. We opened assembly with the school song, and sang 'Land of Hope and Glory'. I suppose I identified very much with being British at that stage. I didn't think particularly of myself as being Irish, I felt these patriotic leaps in my breast when we sang, 'Land of Hope and Glory, Mother of the Free', you know. It was much later when I began to think about what this meant. I remember querying the sort of history and the sort of geography I was being taught, but I didn't get a great response.

I was beginning to be aware of politics – I don't think you can grow up in Belfast without being political. When I was about fourteen or fifteen I joined the Labour League of Youth in Belfast, and I came in contact with some Trotskyists of the Fourth International, and in fact I joined them. I was interested in Russia, and from then on I began to delve more and more into Irish history. There was a place in the wasteland in the middle of Belfast we called 'Red Square', because on Sundays traditionally the little left-wing groups met there and had public meetings. We had the Communist Party on the one bit of waste ground, Trotskyists on the other, and maybe the Labour Party somewhere else. When I was about sixteen I made my first public speech – against the monarchy – in 'Red Square'. In those days everything seemed very clear and simple to me. I thought it was only a question of convincing the good people of the city that this was in their best interests and the revolution would happen tomorrow. But the older I grew . . . .

Around this time, through my political connections, I began to walk up the Falls Road. For a young protestant girl, it was absolutely taboo to go into that area at all. I remember feeling very frightened the first time that I walked up the Falls Road. It was alien to me. I hadn't really been in contact with catholic people ever in my life, but within the Fourth International there were catholics and protestants, and I began to realise that the catholics were also human beings. I know that seems terribly far fetched. To walk up the Falls was very daring as far as I was concerned, and something I wouldn't tell my father and mother about.

One of the boys I knew in the Fourth International – he was a catholic atheist and I was a protestant atheist! – took me to my first céilí in St Mary's Hall, and it was there I met Vincent. He had been interned for three years. He was about twenty-one at the time, I was about seventeen. He was coming towards socialism from republicanism, and of course I was coming to republicanism through socialism, and we sort of collided in the middle. We had a fatal attraction almost. At this time my political life was more important to me than anything else, and it was also my romantic life, because

I started going with Vincent. He was a very romantic figure to me. He had an experience I had no knowledge of. He made me aware of republican life, and Ireland was opening up to me. It became romantic in a very real and emotional way.

I remember the day that I brought Vincent home, and I sat outside on the stairs while my father talked to him. This seems incredible now, but this was what happened. My father was having a man-to-man talk to Vincent. He

A mural in Derry, defaced by the security forces

felt in a terrible dilemma. I'm sure my father and mother were quite heartbroken. I think they were very unhappy about any catholic association, any republican association, and they wanted perhaps to wean me away from this, but at the same time not forbid me. I can appreciate that they had a difficult job; I was a headstrong girl. I was fortunate in that I'd been an only child, that I hadn't realised as a girl that I couldn't do all the things that I wanted to do. I thought of myself as a person, not as a girl or a boy. In a family where the girls had a role to play and the boys had a role to play, I might have accepted that I couldn't do some things, but I was encouraged to think and to read, encouraged to educate myself, if you like. I had a family background of people that had been involved in struggle and I didn't realise it wasn't quite the thing for a girl to do. Of course, Vincent's mother, she was a republican and had been in prison herself. She was devastated that her son was taking up with a protestant. I didn't think then these divides were important. I thought it was quite possible to pass over the bridge, if you like, and I didn't realise just how difficult it was.

Before I met Vincent I hadn't really had any boyfriends. Even at school there was a big divide between the boys and the girls and we didn't really mix or talk to each other very much. It was easier in fact to have a warm loving relationship with a girl than a boy. When I was about fifteen I had a very close friend, and we used to walk about together with our arms round each other. We had a very loving relationship, and it seemed to me a perfectly natural thing to have this really warm relationship. I remember having a crush on a woman teacher, and thinking how beautiful and marvellous she was, and how every word she uttered seemed like pearls. I think that was an emerging sexual feeling if you like. I remember admiring my father very much and loving him, and I remember him having lovely thick curly hair and making curls with my fingers. I remember looking at him walking down the street and thinking how lovely he was and he was my daddy, and really feeling full of love. He was a sort of primary sexual object. I never heard the word lesbian, I don't think I knew what a homosexual was either, I mean that wouldn't have been on my horizon. Sex was a taboo subject. My mother was very sweet and gentle but it was something that she found impossible to talk about, and I wouldn't have mentioned it to my father at all.

I was seventeen when I got pregnant, so that was a bit shattering. And of course, it was shattering for the families. I remember being very sick. I was barely aware that I was pregnant, if you know what I mean, I was sort of trying to blame it on all sorts of things. Then, when I did inevitably find I was pregnant, I was obviously over the moon, excited that there was a life growing inside me. I mean, I may have felt it was inconvenient, and I was not ready for it in many ways, but I was just very pleased I suppose, and Vincent and I were very much in love. Even being political and being perhaps more aware than others, I still thought that as a woman, I would have children, I would get married, have a home, and that was it. I didn't really think of a career.

We decided that we wanted to be married in a registry office, that we didn't want a church wedding at all. It seemed to me the fairest thing anyway, because Vincent was conceding and I was conceding, we were meeting in the middle. This upset his parents, and my parents. His mother couldn't recognise that it was a marriage at all, and my parents thought it was just the lesser of two evils. The only one of my family that came to the wedding was my Auntie Tillie, because, as she confessed to me then, her very first boyfriend had been a catholic, but the family disapproved and she had to give him up. Only Vincent's sister came from his family, so it was very hush hush.

We got a little flat in a house then, privately rented. I remember the night the baby was born. I was out electioneering and the waters broke, so I knew something was happening. I was very excited and very scared too. I went to the hospital, I still didn't have many contractions, or what I call pains, and I was kept waiting during the night. The greatest shock I had was when they shaved my pubic hairs. I was totally unprepared for that, and I felt it was a terrible indignity. I mean, it really shattered me – if anything the birth didn't shatter me, but that did. Then I felt very sick and the nurse wasn't particularly sympathetic. 'Oh, you'll be hours and hours yet,' she said, and she went off. In about ten minutes the baby was born and I was there on my own. I didn't shout or scream because I didn't feel any particular pain, I just felt this sort of 'glug' if you like, and then I was terrified because there was a baby between my legs. I didn't know what to do with it, and was afraid she was going to die. I was just terrified then, and screamed and screamed. They came running up and everything was all right. I hadn't a stitch. The baby was lovely, she was so beautiful. I couldn't get over, you know, how soft and velvety her skin was and how tiny and how perfect her features were. It was ecstasy in that sense. So that was an easy birth.

The day afterwards there was the whole hassle about whether she should be christened or not, but we were very firm. No, the baby wasn't going to be either catholic or protestant. She was going to decide for herself. She was going to be a new Irishwoman. But they could not understand, and I'm sure this was a genuine heartache for Vincent's mother.

Having the young baby, we had to leave our flat and we went to Vincent's mother's house at the bottom of the Falls Road. We had one room we cooked and slept and did everything in. It didn't bother me much at the time. Vincent was still working, I had a lovely baby and I was over the moon. But then, I also discovered that having the baby meant that I wasn't going out any more. Vincent was going out constantly to political meetings. This was about the time when Clann na Phoblachta[7] was beginning to emerge and a few years later the Irish Labour Party was formed, embracing North and South, and we were founder members of that. He was never in because he was a political animal, if you like. But someone had to look after the baby, and it really brought a halt to my activities. But it didn't seem strange or wrong to me at that time. I accepted the role that the woman looked after the child. I don't think Vincent would've known how to change a nappy. I mean, he loved to cuddle the baby when she was cleaned and dressed and fed.

My second daughter was born, and during this time I remember reading D.H. Lawrence's *Sons and Lovers* and *The Rainbow* and books like that, and feeling very much like the woman in that who is completely cocooned in her own fecundity. I was so happy just having babies. It was a very physical pleasure. My whole body was in operation and I felt completely self-contained in myself and my children. I think Vincent was a little apart from that, this was a womanly experience, because men really didn't get that close or involved in the physical sense with the children. The whole business of carrying a child and feeding a child was pleasurable to me. It was a marvellous feeling to be a woman, and I was very, very content with this feeling of being female and producing. Even today, with all the experiences that I have had, I don't think I'll have the total bliss of producing the children, caring for them, again. On another level, as it went on I began to want a more intellectual life, because it was as if my intellectual life was at a complete standstill. So much of your life, when you're dealing with young children, is just keeping the filth at bay, and cooking food, all the physical things, and all very demanding things. At night, I remember, when I got the babies to sleep, I'd lie on the bed and I'd just be so tired, I'd just want to sleep.

My political activity had stopped completely. I mean I was interested, I read as much as I could, I knew what was going on. Vincent was very involved. He would've liked to have been an MP for West Belfast, but of course he was taking a dramatic stand that wasn't acceptable at all. I mean, he had married a protestant, he'd married her in a registry office, he'd two unbaptised children, and he was talking about a socialist republic. You know, it doesn't make for success! During one of the elections in Belfast, he and I were on the platform, supporting the Irish Labour candidate who was up for election in the Falls. One of his opponents got at him through us by spreading the word that we'd been married in a registry office, and we had unbaptised children, so we were literally stoned off the platform. You were acceptable as a catholic communist, or a protestant communist if you like, but you weren't accepted as someone trying to bridge those gaps. Of course, this was a strain on our personal relationship, because all the time there was pressure about the children not being baptised, us not being properly married. I suppose both of us were romantic enough to think we could really move mountains. At that time Vincent also lost his job, and he went down to Dublin and got a job. I was prepared to go to Dublin, because I felt it would give Vincent another chance. He felt he was being discriminated against in Belfast. Surely in Dublin things would be different. So we pulled up all our roots and we went off to Dublin.

I think I disappeared into Dublin a bit. I mean people were nice and friendly and I suppose I was so involved with the kids it didn't matter to me that I had no social contact at all with people. I was used to that in the North. There I never went out for an evening to sit in a home. I never took my children anywhere, because we were not part of the community. I'd no connection with the Catholic Church, I'd no connection with the Protestant Church and there you just have to be one thing or the other, or else you have no social contacts. We were very isolated. I didn't really appreciate that until a bit later on. I don't think I had friends outside the family till I moved to England.

We settled in Dublin, we were very happy there. Vincent was in the Labour Movement there as well, and he was meeting all sorts of people. He stood against Noël Browne in Ringsend constituency and people assumed we were a catholic couple and that the children were baptised. Vincent didn't go out of his way to correct them. But then came the time for our first daughter to start school. There was a catholic school and a protestant school. Vincent took her to the catholic school and they wouldn't take her. I took her to the protestant school and said I wanted her registered as an agnostic and they accepted her. That caused a great uproar with Vincent's mother. 'Protestantism in the South is being allied to England. It can't happen to me and my family. I've been jailed for my republicanism and now you're going to bring my grand-child up as a West Briton.' And of course it was very true. But I said to Vincent, 'Well, one school accepts her as an agnostic, the other doesn't, she's going to the one that accepts her.'

I think I may have been acting out of prejudice as much as he was in fact, I wouldn't be sure of my motives now. The more I delve in the whole business of racism and prejudice, I wouldn't be sure that I hadn't been scarred by my upbringing, if you like. And he was too, because although we could sit down and say we were non-believers and all the rest of it, we were caught up in this whole business of being a catholic or a protestant. The catholicism was the Irish and the protestantism was the English, and in no way could you get away from that. It was a wedge that was being driven between us.

Then Vincent got transferred to County Louth. Now that meant that we had to move back to Omeath, with his mother. My third baby had died when she was only a few months old, and I was pregnant again. I couldn't see any way that I could support myself and the children, or that I could live independently. And I couldn't live off my parents. So I remember just going back to Omeath and accepting the conditions, and the conditions were that the children were baptised and sent to a catholic school. I just said, 'Oh, what the hell, you have to make choices in this life, I suppose if they're catholic and they're Irish ...' but y'see, I didn't see being catholic made you Irish. I felt I was Irish. I was hurt that I wasn't accepted as an agnostic Irish woman, that I had to be a catholic before I'd be accepted as being Irish. I felt I had my traditions too, the '98 tradition, the United Irishmen, and most of them were agnostics anyway. I mean, there was a period of prejudice and bigotry and discrimination shameful to the protestant history, but there was also the tradition in Belfast of the protestants standing guard over the first Catholic Church that was opened in Belfast, the little church at the bottom of the Falls Road, to prevent anything happening to the catholics going to Mass, and that's the tradition I felt I belonged to. I felt bitter that no matter what I was prepared to do for Ireland, I was never going to be Irish, because I was a Northern protestant, and I never felt anything else but that. I suppose I had very strong traditions, I mean traditions of hard work, of non-conformity. I suppose that's what I would say I was, a non-conformist. This came from my parents' background. I don't think anyone can cut off from their family, or their past, or their background. So much of you is made up from how you are reared.

When I was a girl, I thought I only had to give and I'd be accepted, but it's not like that, is it? All I wanted to do was live, live creatively, y'know? That's not much for anybody to ask of life is it? Live in my own way. I've felt that I've always been tolerant of people. If you have a belief I'm not going to infringe on it or demand that you think like me, but I never felt that I had that sort of tolerance for myself.

The children remember the day they were baptised. They were all dressed up. And yet it is something I bitterly regret doing. I really felt that I should've held on, because it didn't solve any problems really, it only created more I think.

After a few years we moved back to Dublin again. By this time I had four children, and I had two more in Dublin. But then, the marriage had gone wrong for more than a year and we agreed that we would be separate and split up, and I would stay in the house and look after the children, but not live as man and wife. But it couldn't work, the emotional pressures were enormous. I remember Vincent lining the children up, he told me nothing in the house was mine, and they were his possessions, it was his house, they were his children. He told them, 'You're not to take any notice of what she says, she's only here to look after you. I'm the one you pay attention to, you listen and do what I tell you.' Some of them remember that to this day. I mean, there were a whole host of things that happened, that we were both to blame for. But the point came that I had to move. When I looked at it very starkly I thought I was going to lose the home, the children. He took three of the children away to his mother's and said he would come back for the others. He tried to pull the baby out of my arms and I wouldn't let him go. He said he would take the children away and that he would leave me without anything. So I fled to England, with as many children as I could. My father was down for a week's holiday at the time, and he gave me some money. I got help from various people.

I went to Reading. I thought I could get some work in a factory and a flat and provide for the kids. We looked all around there, and we came up against these notices: 'No Irish or Coloured'. Somehow I couldn't stand the idea of being there. We stayed on the platform in Reading all night, without shelter, without a place to go to or anything, the three children and I. I mean, that was really an awful experience, of being without a roof over your head and very little money. So we went to London, and I looked up a friend I'd known in my old Fourth International days, and they took us in. They didn't expect me. I walked in on them, but they were very good. We were like refugees. They didn't understand what had happened but they gave us shelter for a week or so, and in that week I got a job. It seems incredible now, only a week. I got this job and accommodation for myself and the baby in a children's home in

Virginia Water. The girls had to stay with friends in London and Wales. It wasn't an easy time.

When I came to England I felt utterly devoid of any personality. I felt that I'd been really reduced to a nothingness, that I'd been utterly scraped out like a shell. I changed my name. I went and had my hair cut. I mean that's nothing really, but I felt a new emerging personality. I'm trying to think back ... I suppose my deepest feeling was the one of needing to survive and needing to cope for the sake of the children. Without children I would've had a nervous breakdown. I always feel that I owe them a tremendous amount, because they gave me a purpose. They gave my life some meaning at a time when the world had come to an end, if you like. I've said this to the girls, that I'm immensely grateful for them being there, because without them I could've just collapsed. They kept me going.

One thing I wasn't sure of until I came to England, until I went to get custody, was the fact that I had no legal right to my own children. I mean, here I was with this feeling of them being so completely mine if you like, and yet suddenly to be told by law they were the father's children. That was only

Family snap of Betty McDowell and some of her family in the 1960s

rectified in England fairly recently, I don't know about Ireland. That was horrifying to me at the time.

I was very aware of my position as a woman because unless I could provide a home for them and support them equally to what Vincent could do in Ireland, I wouldn't even have got custody. We had someone from the courts come out to look at the acommodation, to see how the children were living, what schools they were at. I didn't get any social security or anything else, perhaps I didn't know how to work the system, but also the whole idea of being reliant on social security was somehow anathema to me. I had to prove to myself that I could support my kids. That's why at that time it was so impossible for a woman with children in a difficult situation to go out and try to create a new life and a new home. There were so many barriers, and I'm sure there were a lot of women who would have liked to make an independent stand. I mean, I think I only did it because I was desperate.

I went back as regularly as I could to keep contact with my other children. They weren't allowed to come to my father's house – I had to meet them sometimes in shop door corners, and if I could afford to take them to a hotel, then that was fine. I'm not sure that I could do the same thing again. I'm not totally sure that I could leave them again you know. At that time I was still young, and I still wanted to live, if you like. But I think, looking back on it, the cost to the children was very high, and no matter how long I've been away from them, I've never felt happy about it. I've always felt guilty about it. That will never go away, nor the damage and hurt that was done to the children.

I worked in the children's home for a while, but the whole atmosphere of that home was unhappy. That's when I first decided that I would try and get trained to look after children in some way, and try and give them something more. After that I worked in a Wimpy bar, and then in a launderette and dry cleaners, with a flat above it. It was a beautiful flat, and I was accessible to the girls coming in from school. They could come in and have a cup of tea, and then go up to the flat upstairs. Looking back, we did feel alien. We did hold ourselves together and we often talked about this business of people not understanding what we were laughing at, and we not understanding what they were laughing at. We were very conscious that we were different, we weren't English. But over the years I have become more understanding and more accepting. What I've found in England is a real depth of caring and understanding I didn't experience in Ireland. In Ireland I was really cut off from the two communities and I was isolated. In England, life expanded and opened out, and there was all sorts of directions I could go in, and all sorts of contacts with people that I just never had in Ireland. So I have had a lot here.

When the girls left school, I went to college, to train to be a teacher. I got a grant of £500 a year I think it was, and that was absolutely amazing – somebody handing me money! But it was a very hard time – the whole experience of coming up to London and living in one room without my children, who were all off doing their own thing – I really felt very lonely. I found it hard to be on my own in the evenings. Again, you know, it was one of those situations where you keep yourself alive by exploring new possibilities, a new part of yourself, don't you? In one sense it was very lonely, but an exciting and developing time. Then I met Ted – that was almost ten years after I'd left Ireland – and when I met him I was ready for a relationship with a man. Before that, I'd had it up to there, you know! The relationship just gathered strength from year to year. It was very fortunate, I suppose I was able to decide that I could do what I liked then, at that stage.

I was teaching by the time I had another daughter and I gave it up for a while, but I found it very difficult to be in the position of not earning my own money. I was determined that I would never be without my independence. I really couldn't, I felt too insecure and too vulnerable. When she was four and a half I got this present job. I work alongside bi-lingual children in the classroom helping them to develop their command of English. I've been doing this work for the past eight or nine years.

I always wanted to teach immigrant children, because I felt I could empathise with their need to survive in an alien society. One of the most enriching things about the job is the women I meet. The Muslim, Hindu, black women, who maybe have had some difficulties in coping with a new society, but also have a tremendous amount of strength that their experiences have given them. Over the next few months I will be involved in racism awareness training for teachers, and I feel that this is tremendously important work. I think it goes right back to my life in Belfast, because you *can* reject your own community if it's not behaving properly. White people can do this if they want to.

The more I look back on my life, the more I think it could be so many women's experience. It was very hard then for a woman to leave just because she was unhappy – it put you into poverty, into a position where you had to accept poverty. A lot of people have found that out since. But then, I think, life is always only beginning, isn't it?

Notes

1. A strike against the cutting of relief at a time of very high unemployment. Organised by the Unemployed Workers' Movement, it was supported by catholics and protestants.
2. A protestant society, set up in Armagh in 1795 against a background of agitation of catholic emancipation. It aimed to protect protestant ascendancy and interests. It spread rapidly throughout Ulster and continues today to be the backbone of loyalism.
3. A socialist song.
4. A republican song.
5. A loyalist song.

6. An armed rebellion by the United Irishmen which was defeated in 1798. The United Irishmen, founded by the protestant Wolfe Tone and others in 1791, aimed for reforms based on the principles of civil, political and religious liberty. Wolfe Tone was influenced by Thomas Paine and the French revolutionaries, and is referred to as 'the father of Irish republicanism'.
7. Clann na Phoblachta was founded in 1946 as an opposition party to the left of Fianna Fail. It was a member of the inter-party government after the 1948 general election.

No Irish Need Apply

A roof over our heads

This interview centres on the first few years of Una Cooper's life in England. After selling up her house in Dublin, she arrived with four small children, to join her husband. She describes the ordeals they went through in their search for decent housing.

Before we were married, Bill wanted me to go to Australia and I said, 'No.' Who wants to leave their Mum? I never wanted to leave my Mum. I didn't want to leave my Mum to get married. I couldn't picture being away from her. But after we were married a few years and things got tight, Bill said, 'I'm going to pack it up. I'm going to London. I'll go on my own.' Oh, I felt awful. I felt terrible. Well, I knew I couldn't go and bring my children to nothing. He'd have to go and find a place for us.

So he went off, and from the day he left I used to write a letter every day. I used to start the letter in the evening time, at five o'clock – like a diary I used to write it. I put the times on it and I used to put, 'Got up, children went up to the school, he did this, he did that, baby has a tooth.' I'd write it out as a diary all the time. Then I used to run up every second day and post it, in a post box up at Manor Street. And every Thursday he used to post me my money.

It took him a year, or just over a year . . . I remember, it was in August 1954 he said to me, 'I've got a place for us.' I was so thrilled. And then I thought, I'm not going to London. When he comes home, when he sees the place – I'll have it all done up – he'll change his mind. But when he came he said 'I've got a garden flat in Regent's Park Road and the landlord said we can have it for as long as we like. It's all arranged, I've given in some money, and he's holding it open for us.'

I felt all mixed up. I felt mixed up because I loved Dublin. I still love Dublin though it's not my Dublin anymore, you know, it's changed so much. But we came here anyway, the flat was lovely and we were getting on quite well. If Bill didn't like the job, he could walk out of it at eleven o'clock and be in a different one by twelve. He could walk from job to job, he was never idle really for more than a couple of hours.

The first Sunday we were here, we found out where the church was and where the school was, they were the main things. But it was a terrible shock not knowing anyone. Nobody speaks to you in London, they really don't speak to you. It's a cold, cold place really when you come here. My children were too tiny. I had four – my eldest was five, the youngest was fourteen months. We were a little thing on our own.

I can't remember how long we'd been in this place, say two years, or something like that, when one day I'm lying in bed ill and the landlord walks in. He turns the key, he hands me this notice, and walks out. Although he was the landlord, he used to turn the key and walk in. I'm in the bed, it's a notice to quit, and I'm thinking 'Oh, my God!' I'm in a dreadful state of panic.

So from that night on, when Bill came in from work, the children were in bed, they were always in bed by half past six, I'd everything done, Bill's dinner was on the table and I'd get up and go out. I'd have read the local paper for adverts. I'd have gone to shop windows but always – 'No Coloured or Irish need apply'. It was Houses to let, Flats to let, Rooms to let, but every one of them 'No Irish or Coloured need apply'. So I thought, I'll present myself at their doors. But when they'd hear my accent some of them would say, 'It's gone.' Of course, I had no bus fare or anything. I would have to walk. I would go anyway but no way would they take children. I went everywhere. Bill couldn't do it because he was the breadwinner. He had to keep the work going. I wasn't clued up about the councils and all that. I forgot who it was now that I went to, and they said, 'The only thing you can do is to go to the police.' So I went to the police station and I said, 'What does one do, I have children.' They said, 'The only thing you can do is the day that you've got to be out of that house, you come along to the police station. You present yourself to the police with your children, and they will get you something.'

So, we packed all these suitcases, only what we could carry. We had to leave everything else. We went to the police station, and they said, 'You take the train, get off the train, get on to such a bus, you go there, we ring them, and you're to present yourself there.' Anyway, we arrived in this place, about four miles away from Elephant and Castle, and to me it looked dreadful. The outside was like a prison, and a warden or someone let us in the gate. We were brought into this huge big awful dining hall, and this woman came to us. She was like a matron or something, she had a uniform on, and she said, 'I'm very sorry, Mr Cooper, but we only take mothers and children here. Men are not

142

allowed.' Well, we were devastated, you know, we didn't know what to do. I couldn't describe it, it's horrifying now even for me to think about it. And all the children were getting tired by now. They wanted to go to bed. They wanted to go home. So, I started crying.

Anyway, they brought us up to a room. This was the nicest room she could get me, she said. It was a dormitory, there was about five women in it, and loads of screaming children and noise everywhere. Just iron beds up against a wall, and she said, 'Take those.' I think they gave the boys tops and tails and I know we took up five, or four beds along the wall.

We came down the next morning to this dreadful big dining-room, and there were children running up and down the table, urinating on the table and dirty old men coming in then. I think they used to let them in for their breakfast or something. Women, dreadful looking characters, children with sores on their heads. Then this man sent for me. I'd say he was the governor, like in a prison. And he looked up at me and he said, 'I find it very distressing to see a woman like you in a place like this. It's no place for you to be.' So I said, 'Well, what's the answer for it?' 'I don't really know at the moment,' he said, 'but I'll do what I can for you.' Later on in the morning, this woman came looking for me and she said, 'Come with me, dear.' She opened this door and it was like a cubbyhole. 'He has asked me to get you somewhere away on your own, with your little family,' she said, 'I know you won't be able to move in here, but it's the best we can do for you, because we feel that you shouldn't be with anyone else.' So I was absolutely delighted, even with this. We were

Una Cooper

143

on top of each other, we couldn't move. The kids had to sit up on their beds all the time, you know. Bill was allowed to come and see me at night time, and he used to bring me half of the sandwich that he had in the daytime, because I couldn't eat anything down in this dining-room. And the amount they were charging us was nearly what Bill was going to get in wages!

I won't go into details about the horrible place it was, and the conditions. I couldn't tell you ... a workhouse, although it was run by the council. The food used to come up and they would slap it on to a plate. There were mugs, tin mugs. It was dreadful. When I asked, 'Can my baby have a boiled egg?' I was told, 'Oh no, only pregnant women can have an egg.' I mean, Bill used to run the Morning Star hostel in Belfast, I was in the Legion of Mary at home, so we were always involved, but I thought, the worst day I ever saw the poor tramps coming into Dublin, I've never seen anything like this.

I didn't think it was having as much effect on the boys as it was on me and the baby, Sheila. She was showing it so much. Every week when I went to the doctor I'd say, 'What about my baby? She's not eating.' They used to keep saying to me, 'She's a normal child, there's nothing wrong with her. If all the children here were as healthy and as normal as her, they'd be all right.' I couldn't believe that. Then one Saturday I had Sheila in my arms, and I'm walking up and down with her and I'm crying and I'm looking at her. I've already said in the morning, 'My child is getting worse, she is ill. I don't care what you say.' And all of a sudden I feel her spitting out, and I get such a panic. Oh, God. She's going to die. This sister comes down and I said, 'Look at my baby, *look at my baby now*, what are you going to do about it?' And she said, 'Oh, my God, why didn't you call me before. Why didn't you tell us about this child?' So an ambulance comes and takes her down to a hospital in Surrey. And she's telling me in her baby language don't leave her, but you see she's whipped away anyway into an isolation ward and we're not allowed to see her until Sunday morning. I didn't visit an awful lot because I was so heart-broken. She would just stand there with her arms up in the air and say, 'Take me, take me, take me.' That's all she'd say to me, poor child. It took a while before she got better.

Eventually this governor sent for me and said, 'Mrs Cooper, I can't bear to see you like this. I want you to lift that phone and speak to Dublin, and there will be a house waiting for you in Dublin, a Corporation house. We'll pay your fares to go back.' And I thought, 'I've sold my home, I've nothing, what am I going back to? Nothing.' So I said, 'No, I'm not going back now. Everything has gone. My home has gone. I've nothing left. I'm going to make a life for myself here, I'm not going back.' And that really made me angry, to think that he could get me a Corporation house in Dublin to walk into, and they'd pay my fare, after going through all this. So they put me on a list for short stay accommodation and told me they would get me out of there as quick as they could. I think we were out of there in – I think it was three months. We were told that we were going to a short stay accommodation, where you were again with a crowd of people. You had communal kitchens, but your own sleeping accommodation. We were there another year and a half, I think it was. Oh, you couldn't get a place, there's no way you could get a place, once you had children. I mean, even if you had two children they wouldn't let you in, and once you were Irish, once they heard the accents, that was it. They didn't want you, they just didn't.

I never moved the children from their schooling, I thought to do that would be really bad. They needed something stable so we kept that, no matter what hardship. Then my doctor said to me, 'You can't go on like this. You know what's going to happen? Your children are going to be taken away from you, if you go under now. They'll all be taken away, and,' he said, 'this would be a dreadful tragedy. So, I'm writing to Camden.' He persecuted Camden and one day he picked up the phone and spoke to the Town Hall and said, 'I'm not going to be put off anymore. If you haven't got a place for this woman within the next twenty-four hours, you will hear all about it, and it won't be on the phone. Now get your finger out,' he said, 'and do something for this woman right away.' And do you know, within twenty-four hours I was offered a house. And when we went up to see it I couldn't believe it, you know, I just couldn't believe we'd got it.

Nobody back home in Dublin knew what I went through. I never told any of them at the time because I knew it would worry them. Afterwards I told them. It changed me enormously, living here. My idea would be, maybe this is very strange to hear, for every person that's at home in Ireland, that they should come over and serve two years' apprenticeship in London to find out what it's like, and they would be different people, better people, in every way.

Manchester Childhood, 1930s

A strong feeling for roots

Born of Irish parents in Manchester in the 1930s, Anne Higgins describes the two major cultural influences in her life, and her changing sense of identity over time.

We were under a kind of sense of siege being Irish catholics in Manchester in the thirties and forties. We lived initially in a very poor inner-city district where there were many other Irish families. The parish school we went to had mainly Irish teachers and pupils, we knew Irish catholic families in the street, we met Irish people at the church, and we didn't have to associate with English people if we didn't want to. In point of fact, my mother made friends easily and a next door neighbour who was a very staunch English protestant became her best friend in no time, but we mixed mainly with other Irish people.

I suppose it was our accents but mainly our religion which set us apart from the rest. We went to Mass on Sunday morning and stayed at home on Sunday afternoon. The protestant children went to Sunday school on a Sunday afternoon and their parents had the tradition of going to bed on a Sunday afternoon to have a rest. In those days a lot of the people from around the place were doing hard physical work – from six in the morning till late at night – and all these catholic kids would be bashing around the street playing noisy ball games and the windows would be going up telling us in no uncertain terms to go away and be quiet ... so there was that clash. Then going to and from school in a big group, we would be travelling in opposite directions and we would call out 'Proddie Dogs' while they'd call 'Cat Licks'. They might run at us and chase us but nothing serious. It was just the usual kind of them and us, gangs, you know, and we gave as good as we got. Another thing was that they had different holidays off. We had the Holy Days of Obligation and St Patrick's Day. They had Empire Day and Guy Fawkes Day and you would go and look through the railings of the local C. of E. school when they were having fun and games which you were a bit jealous of but at the same time despised. My mother would never let us, even if we could have afforded the uniform, join the Girl Guides or the Boy Scouts because that was English and protestant as far as she was concerned.

St Patrick's Day in the parish was definitely a great day and our equivalent of Empire Day. There would be Mass in the morning and in the evening a great gathering of the clans at the Free Trade Hall for a concert. We all wore shamrock – a great lapelful which I wouldn't do now because I don't believe in any kind of nationalism to that extent these days – but at that time it was the right thing to do because you felt threatened and a minority and didn't want to be ashamed of the fact, so it was the natural thing to do. Because people were anti-catholic and anti-Irish, you tended to go out of your way to assert the fact that you were proud of being Irish and catholic whenever the opportunity arose.

The Jews and the catholics in Manchester were in the same ghetto in the north, Cheetham Hill Road, and they were very much sympathetic towards each other as minorities. We had Jewish girls at school, I had a friend who was Jewish, my mother worked for a local doctor who was a Dublin Jew and our doctor was an Irish Jew, from Limerick. One of the great Jewish heroes of the post-war years, as far as we were concerned, was Leslie Lever, a Labour MP who had grown up in St Edmund's parish amongst the Irish. He was also Lord Mayor of Manchester and made a great issue of being pro-catholic/Irish. He used to head the catholic parade. We had these Whit Sunday parades, you know, catholics walked Friday, protestants walked Monday to the centre of the city and Leslie Lever was always on the catholic parade. He was considered the 'Mr Fixit' for the catholics.

Both my parents were Irish. My mother was from Kildare and though my father had actually been born in Manchester, he was backwards and forwards to Ireland a lot as a child, had an Irish accent, and would have described himself very much as Irish. They married in Dublin but moved over here in 1928. I was two weeks old when I first went to Ireland and I held a grudge against my mother for not making a different arrangement so that I could have been born there! My sister, who was born in Ireland, used to tease me about not being really Irish and my father used to console me. My father was a republican, so he told me lots of stories about 1916, the Civil War, Michael Collins and other people whom he'd met when he was in Dublin. That was the high point of his life probably, that exciting period between 1912–1928 and he talked a lot about it. He was a great storyteller naturally and he told us stories every night when he took us to bed. My mother did the same thing but to a lesser extent. He used to sing Irish songs. He knew them all by heart back to the Middle Ages, you know, so we grew up with a repertoire of Irish ballads and songs.

He was in the Manchester branch of the Gaelic League and a socialist, like his father before him, at a time when the British Establishment was very anti-socialist. For generations they'd been left-wing as a result of the poverty in Ireland that they saw around them, I suppose. After the war he became an active member of the Anti-Partition League, at a time when many people had forgotten the North of Ireland still existed as a problem. But he was in no way anti-British. That was also true of my mother. She was also sympathetic to Irish nationalism but made us aware of the violent and tragic side as well as the romantic side. My father never mentioned any IRA killings or anything of that kind, but my mother's mother knew stories going back generations to the Whiteboys,[1] you know, and of the atrocities committed on both sides.

Looking back on it, I suppose there was a difference in the kinds of stories my mother and father told. It's only since I've thought about it that I've realised this difference. My father's stories were mainly about the 1916 and 1922 events and Irish history from way back, whereas my mother's stories were about her family, her brothers and sisters, her aunts and uncles, her great-aunts and grandmother. She talked about what great-aunt Lucy did and what Aunt Julia did and her stories were all concerned with families. It was she who kept in close contact with our relatives and who invited our cousins to stay when they first came over to find work. My father relied on my mother to even send cards to his relatives at Christmas.

After the war, when we were a bit older, my mother joined the Women's Co-operative Movement and the Labour Party. She used to go for weekend courses and have to read accounts of things or take minutes or become a member of a committee or something like that, and that gave her a lot of self-confidence.

My mother and us children visited Ireland almost annually. I spent a year there when I was four years old because my grandmother was very ill and my mother went to look after her. Then I spent a year there at the outbreak of the war, as an alternative to evacuation. I loved being in the country. My aunt had quite a big farm which she inherited from a prosperous gentleman farmer for whom she'd worked as a housekeeper. We used to spend our day driving around on the carts. The farmhands used to put us up on the horses and up on the back of the binding machine and give us rides in wheelbarrows and that kind of thing, so we thought it was great.

I went to the local National School. I was terribly aware of the poverty of the farmhands' children there. TB was rife and children were dying of meningitis – there were no classmates that died in England that I remembered. My aunt would say, 'Don't go with that one, they're consumptives, don't play with them, they're consumptives.' Well, if they weren't consumptives, they

Anne Higgins

weren't clean, they had head lice or something like that, so you ended up with nobody to play with if you followed the instructions to the letter. There was terrible poverty, because the farm labourers' pay was very, very low. I mean, it was very bad at home in Manchester because my father didn't qualify for unemployment benefit. But it seemed worse to me in Ireland. It seemed very noticeable that a large number of children didn't wear shoes at all during the summer months right into the cold weather, you know. They'd usually have boots in the winter time but they'd have to walk long distances to school and all they brought with them each day was a wedge of unbuttered soda bread and a small medicine bottle full of milk. I can remember on one occasion a child riding around a water trough and he fell off his bike and a milk bottle broke and cut the sole of his foot. It was very badly cut and the headmaster took him on the crossbar to the local nurse and then he got to a doctor. There were no cars and we were miles from anywhere. I remember taking my own shoes and socks off and hiding them in a ditch at the back gate on the way to school to be the same as the others. Our family might be the only ones in summer time wearing shoes, in fact.

They teased me about my accent, the children in England and Ireland – in both schools. They would stand around you in the playground and say, 'Say this, say that,' and they were impressed by your accent. I rather wanted to stay in Ireland. I became very fond of my aunt when I went to stay with her on my own, and I was spoilt there, you see. Being the only child in the household, I was the centre of attraction so I rather did want to stay. But as soon as I got home, in no time I was back into the swing of home life once more.

It was soon after my return to Manchester that my sister and I began to attend the Gaelic League. On Saturday afternoon they had children's dance classes and then, as you went into adolescence, we went to the Gaelic League for a céilí on a Sunday night. That was a regular part of my social life. They had language classes and a choir and rambles up to the Pennines in the summer, and things of that kind. But by no means the majority of the Irish went to the Gaelic League. It was the very pro-Irish ones who went. There were differences between members of the same family in how far they identified themselves as Irish as well. It's very hard to pin down why. I suppose it's to do with your personality and how you identify. I had a very strong attachment to my father and certainly I retained an interest in it all.

As a child, the catholic and Irish thing were absolutely intertwined. Very much so. At school most of the nuns and the lay teachers were Irish. The nuns had a strong belief in the importance of education for women and gave us a lot of encouragement. I don't remember learning any Irish history in school though. In secondary we learned British history in the 1800s and therefore we learned about Home Rule, but we used British textbooks. I can't remember any particular statement in the book that I thought was totally wrong, just that it didn't give the whole story, or deal with the complexities of the issue. We had an Irish nun who taught history who was herself a great storyteller and would easily divert us from the subject in hand to tell a story about O'Connell or Parnell. She would let me stand up and argue against anything in the book. I felt it was important to do that because I did the same thing in our house. I liked an argument, my father had taught me as an infant that it was a game to argue. Because the environment was very Irish I was safely cocooned in the school. We felt sorry for the English catholics, few and far between as they were, and they certainly felt overwhelmed by us. They were definitely the minority.

As we came to adolescence there was a lot of anxiety about you marrying a non-catholic. The priest used to get up on the pulpit once a month giving this reminder. If I had time I could remember it by heart: 'Young people are warned against forming friendships with non-catholics. If such a friendship has been formed it either has to be broken off or . . .' Our Bishop was very conservative and old-fashioned. If you married a non-catholic in the thirties and up to the beginning of the forties, you could no longer teach in a catholic school. This was considered even then to be somewhat extreme but we all accepted that a mixed marriage would bring problems, particularly for children. I went along with it, I suppose. I didn't feel critical, I accepted it. It either matters or it doesn't. In the same way that I wouldn't dream of marrying a Conservative, I wouldn't have thought of marrying a non-catholic. If you had the same background, same interests, same attitudes, I felt this would be very helpful to a marriage. We didn't talk about sex. No, no. It was not talked about except if you heard of anybody's daughter expecting a baby before marriage. It was regarded as a tragedy and something to be avoided at all costs. Contraceptives we knew nothing about, except that they were forbidden. That was the Church's teaching and it was accepted. As far as sex was concerned you knew you had to go to Confession once a month and that was the thing that was upmost in your mind, whenever temptation struck, you know.

I went to a single sex girls' school and there were very few of us who went out socially and had boyfriends then. Not many of our parents had had secondary education so they constantly reminded us how lucky we were to be at that school, what a privilege it was, how we had these God-given talents and had to use them. You knew you'd passed your eleven plus and it was a waste of the public's mone if you didn't pass your exams so you had a lot of homework to do up until the sixth form. If you worked in a factory you might have had boyfriends but people in grammar schools . . . it wasn't expected of you! Going to the céilís once a week was permissible though.

My family kept in touch with events in Ireland. During the war we were conscious of Churchill's anti-Irish attitude. My father was quite pro-Dev but he didn't think much of any of them. It wasn't what he would have liked to happen in Ireland after 1922. So, he thought Dev was well within his rights to stay neutral and it was very understandable. He thought they ought to bargain about the North perhaps. I remember Churchill said something very anti-Irish in some speech in connection with Irish neutrality, that they were more or less pro-fascist in not letting them have the ports. But there wasn't a great deal more the Irish could have done except give the use of the ports. They were providing food and labour for the war effort. My brother was in the British Army, my first cousin was in the WAAFS and lots more came over to work in munitions factories and things of that kind.

Just after the war then, my parents and many other Irish people were active politically in the Catholic Parents and Electors Association. Most Irish were Labour, most of the Irish we knew were very mildly left-wing, but not many of them were active, except in this Association. It was very important after the new Butler Education Act in 1944.[2] There was a great deal of anxiety on the part of the hierarchy at that time that they were going to lose control of the catholic schools. They wanted to retain some control so they paid a certain amount towards the building costs rather than accept 100 per cent grants from the state. The Catholic Parents and Electors Association was set up to ensure that whatever happened with the new Education Act, the catholics would keep control of the catholic schools. Both my parents were involved in that. But they were very much trying to put over the fact that it wasn't socialists you had to be afraid of. The Church's attitude was, that if a Labour government got in, it would be terrible, you know. But, my parents were trying to point out that they voted Labour, and they were still wanting to retain the catholic schools, that there was no anomaly in that, that you could be pro Labour and pro catholic schools simultaneously.

After leaving school, I went to train as a teacher at a catholic college in Prestwick. We wouldn't have dreamed of going anywhere else, nobody in the school went to a non-catholic one. If you wanted to teach in catholic schools, you had to have your Catholic Religious Education teaching certificate. I continued to visit Ireland in that period after I left school but not so often. I went with my mother on one occasion and with my friend from school who was doing a thesis at university on O'Casey, and I went with her to show her around Dublin.

After a few years' teaching in Manchester, I moved down to St Albans in 1959. It's a small town, a market centre and commuter town for London. There's very little manufacturing industry, most people are employed in services. Pre-war, there were very few Irish here and there was quite a bit of prejudice against them I think, from what I've heard. It's changed very much now but the Irish were few and far between then and very much aliens. It wasn't like the north of England where they'd been used to them for generations. The Irish community is still fairly small but people came out after the war from London and there were quite a number who came to work in Luton or on the motorway, who then moved to St Albans. There are three big mental hospitals as well as the City Hospital and there are quite a lot of nursing staff who are Irish. I was conscious of quite a lot of differences between north and south when I moved down. Especially in relation to casual meetings I had with people in the street or in buses. But because I moved from a catholic school in Manchester to a catholic school here and the nuns were all Irish practically and many of the staff were Irish catholics, I was cocooned again by a number of people to whom I could relate easily.

My first contact down here outside that environment was the Labour Party, and I met quite a few non-catholics there. There weren't many Irish in the Labour Party which was surprising to me after Manchester, where most of the catholic Irish I'd known were Labour voters. I always felt that the issue of Ireland was low down on the Labour Party's priorities. It was always something that they were sympathetic about but never got around to doing anything about. They didn't know or understand much about it down here. I remember in the early 1960s, during one election period, I was canvassing for the Labour candidate – actually wasting my time – but I can remember an old Irish lady coming into the Labour Rooms and saying she was going to all the party headquarters to enquire about their views on gerrymandering and the denial of civil rights to catholics in Northern Ireland and was voting accordingly. Our candidate thought she was a maniac, you know, and that she'd got a bee in her bonnet. He'd never given the matter a moment's thought. But because I was there, I was able to talk knowledgeably about it to her and she was suitably impressed and she promised she'd vote for him! They hadn't a clue about it; it just didn't impinge upon their consciousness at all. The level of ignorance I think is partly due to the press and also it's similar to the north/south divide. I have spoken to people since I've been down here about the thirties and they've said that they weren't aware of any depression in the thirties. They were very well off, and everybody they knew had jobs and they thought it was all exaggerated. They'd never experienced the poverty. I'm still a member of the Labour Party but rarely do anything other than address envelopes at local election time.

I met my husband here. He moved down to teach after I did. In fact, he was at the same primary school as me and his grandfather was Irish. We had friends and acquaintances in common even before we met. I've a strong feeling for roots myself and I was glad that we both had the same kind of background and beliefs. I, myself, have experienced very little anti-Irish prejudice. People don't know I'm Irish unless I refer to the fact – which I very quickly would do – but I don't have an Irish accent or a very Irish name. I remember when I went to Ireland as a child and was teased for my English accent. People would say, 'You're not Irish, you're not Irish.' That used to annoy me more than anything that has happened to me here. It has been anti-catholic feeling that I encountered more. Some Labour Party members here were very anti-catholic and anti-church schools but that was not really anti-Irish. I don't mind the jokes about the Irish on television. They don't bother me because they are so very exaggerated that I couldn't take offence, anyway. If I heard them told by somebody who was normally racially prejudiced, who I felt really meant it, then I certainly would be offended. But I'm not usually.

153

I suppose anti-Irish jokes might have a negative effect on children born here. I have heard pupils at school talking about their parents being Irish and how they feel their parents are pushing them into listening to Irish music while they want to listen to pop music. They are turned off by their parents' over-anxiety to retain their culture, and a sense of their own roots. But I think in adolescence it often changes, they want to be themselves and get bored by constant references to Ireland.

At the school I teach in there are first and second generation Irish. The degree to which they identify with their Irish heritage varies enormously. We don't have St Patrick's Day as a holiday now and very few wear shamrock. Well, partly because 50 per cent of the staff are not catholic and certainly not Irish and there are fewer whose parents want that. The parents who do want Irish culture send their children to play in Irish bands or to the Comhaltas[3] to do Irish dancing or to Gaelic football. But it's all done through the parents, outside school.

I suppose my sense of Irishness has distanced over time and that's inevitable. It's diluted, if you like. It isn't that I feel less Irish but that I feel more interested in individuals and whether I can be on the same wavelength as them or not. So I have lots of friends who are not Irish and I go to Ireland less often. I would feel in a roomful of Irish people that I identified with them, but that they wouldn't necessarily want to include me in an inner circle. They would see me as different. If I had to choose between being Irish and English, I probably would say, 'I'm Irish.' But, I would definitely count myself as Irish if I felt I was among people who were anti-Irish, and if there was any question of prejudice I would immediately have something to say about it. I believe that people should always rejoice in what they've gained from their own culture and also try to learn from others. Nowadays I go to an occasional céilí, but I'm not a member of anything. Also, I've been looking after my mother since she moved down to live and she's not been well – so I've practically given up parish activities.

I don't have children of my own but I feel part of a bigger family. I have nieces and nephews and cousins and their children, you know, and there's quite an Irish element to all that. Irish people invest an awful lot in their children, they are very important in the family as is this sense of the family over generations – it's more like the extended family. My own aunts were very important to me, they didn't have children of their own, and I had a maiden aunt who was a very important person in the family. I feel fortunate to belong to an extended family clan.

Being a catholic has remained important, too. Perhaps because I went from school to a catholic college, from there to a catholic school to teach, and I've taught religion and continued to live and work amongst catholics most of my adult life. I don't mean to say that I would be totally uncritical of the Church's teaching or past record in dealing with poverty, or the way many of them have identified themselves more with the privileged establishment and made no stand against the injustices being suffered by the poor. I wouldn't be without criticism of them. And because we had some protestant ancestry who'd become catholics, I was never brought up to be anti-protestant.

As far as the Church's teaching on contraception and sex generally is concerned, it's terribly difficult to draw the line between giving people a terrible sense of unnecessary guilt, and being so tolerant as to condone promiscuity and all the unhappiness that that can bring, particularly to children, with broken marriages. I think the Church hasn't been good at finding that balance. Though it is now acknowledged that decisions about contraception within marriage are a matter of individual conscience ultimately. The more scientific knowledge we gain about human fertility, the more difficult are the ethical problems we have to face. But I think we do have to make a stand against what we consider to be wrong in principle. I would regard abortion to be morally reprehensible. I could never do it. But I don't think we can condemn individuals who do it while as a community we don't offer support to single parents and the parents of handicapped children. There's no doubt in my mind that the 1960s sexual revolution has created more problems than it solved. Social pressures on teenagers to have sex before they are mature causes a great deal of stress.

My religion, political beliefs and national identity were all inter-related when I was a child. I've had to rethink my position on all of these over the years but I'm glad I have been able to carry with me much of what was important to me as a child.

Notes

1. Whiteboys appeared in Limerick in 1761 when landlords first tried to enclose common land. They carried out acts of resistance and revenge in the land agitation of the following years. They disguised themselves by wearing their shirts over their clothes, hence their name.
2. The 1944 Education Act provided for free, universal education up to school-leaving age, and a common curriculum. Religious denominations feared that a Labour government would further erode their power to control their own schools.
3. An organisation to promote Irish culture with branches in Ireland and Britain.

Work

Morning, noon and night

Joan Doherty, a childminder for the past ten years

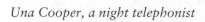
Una Cooper, a night telephonist

Below: Margaret O'Reilly, who has been in nursing since 1949
Bottom: Eileen Doherty, a teacher

Ann Rice, a senior clerical officer, at work on payday in a home help office

Post Office queue, Monday, 8.50 a.m.

Karen Doherty, home from school washing up

Below: May Kehoe, a hospital domestic who has worked in the Health Service for most of her thirty-five years here

Bottom: Fiona MacNeely.   Opposite: Mary Hegarty has been designing and making Irish dancing costumes for fourteen years. Her embroidery is based on the Book of Kells.

Cec Houlihan, a self-employed painter and decorator

Anne Woods, a district nurse who trained when her children reached school age

Bridie Fox, one of the few women chief stewards with British Rail

Around the clock picket to oppose hospital closure in Neasden, North London

Rose-Anne Varley, a community psychiatrist who trained in Ireland

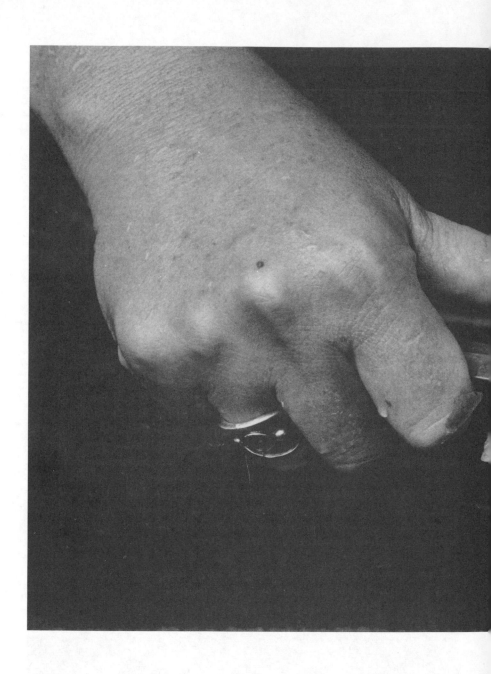

Nobody knew how you did it

Nancy Lyons left Kerry in February 1943 after working on the family farm for a number of years. Here she describes some of the hidden labours of women's lives.

I was the eldest of three brothers and four sisters, and we lived on a small farm near Farranfore, in Kerry. When I left school at fourteen, I didn't look for a job. The girls who would have got jobs would all have gone to secondary school and I hadn't. I stayed for six years and, as we used to say, worked at home – inside and outside. The farm wasn't so big, but in those days you did a bit of everything. You went to the creamery every day so you had your creamery cheque; if you kept fowl, the eggs were sold; you did a lot of hay, so there was hay to be sold in the winter when there would be no other money coming in.

It was hard work. Let's say a typical summer day I'd be up between six and half-six in the morning. We had a very long journey to the creamery which used to take three hours, so my father, my mother and myself would milk the cows. Then I'd go to the creamery at about half-past-seven, and I'd be home about half-past ten. Then I used to mow, you know, drive the horses to mow a field of corn, or perhaps there'd be a field of hay down. Then home again – water was always a terrible job with us, it was very scarce, there was no supply, so water often had to be drawn if you had a dry season. Anything like this, all day, until my mother would call us to the dinner – then out again until it was time to milk the cows in the evening. If it was fine weather you wouldn't start to milk until about half-past six in the evening, so you finished that about eight o'clock perhaps. Then there were the chores, there was lots of chores to be done after, you know. You probably wouldn't finish till nine o'clock or half-past.

My brothers and sisters were all going to different schools, so there were meals continuously as well – a dinner for each one coming in at different times. They didn't have school meals or anything, of course. I was the only body at home now, apart from my father and mother, who was gainfully employed – if you'd call it gainfully employed. And thruppence on a Sunday night to go into the dance was your gainful employment!

I had a cousin, a priest, who spent a lot of time in our house, and we were fairly compatible. This particular summer, which would be the summer of '42, he took me to one side and he gave me a long talk. He said, 'The only thing I can see for you at the end of your days is having a load of cats around you. You're going to stay until you are so old nobody else is going to want you. They're all going to go away.' 'But,' I said, 'what can I do?' 'Oh, rubbish,' he said, 'of course there's loads you can do.'

I had an uncle of my father's who was here in England and so I decided to write to him and ask him to get me into a hospital. He wrote back and said he would gladly look for a place for me, but it was war time. He very kindly offered to pay the fee for me if I preferred to get into a hospital in Ireland. I weighed the pros and cons and I said to my mother, 'Supposing I don't do any good. Supposing they throw me out and he has paid a fee, I'm always going to feel obligated. I'll take my chance and I'll go away, if he can get me into somewhere.' So he got the papers, and I applied to the London County Council and they gave me a place at Paddington Hospital, Harrow Road. This was in 1943, before the National Health Service.

It took two days' travelling, in the month of February. I travelled from Farranfore to Dublin. At Mallow we changed trains and I got talking to two girls who went to school with my sister. They were going to the same hospital, Paddington Hospital, Harrow Road, so naturally that threw the three of us together. We stayed in Dublin overnight and I always claim that had I not met them, instead of going to Dun Laoghaire on the following morning, I would have gone to Kingsbridge station instead! I'd had enough of travelling by the time I got to Dublin – believe me, by the time I got to Killarney I'd had enough!

Anyway, we got on the boat – I've a vague remembrance of this awful old cattle boat. We got to Holyhead and got the train down to Euston. It was a very strange experience, all the soldiers and everything on the train. Then, of course, as it got dark while we were travelling the black-out blinds were drawn. All this perhaps prepared us a little bit for what was in store ... we were so innocent going to England.

When we arrived at the hospital it was late and the night sister met us in the hall. She said, 'Hello nurses.' We had just put our foot inside, you see, and we were nurses straight away, under the command! I got a lovely room, my own, and I was thrilled. Mind you, by the time the next day was over it had all worn off, but at first it seemed all lovely. I got to my room and sat down straight away and wrote pages of a letter to my mother. I told her about the lovely room I had and everything!

We were very protected really. I think they did have a conception of the young girl leaving home for the first time, y'know. There was such a lot of staff looking after you, who were very protective towards you. They were really very patient people, and they were very good. They made sure you had your meals, and when the air raid siren went, made sure you were all right and all this kind of thing.

It was very different to today, I suppose, because you only went for a month into the preliminary training scheme. You were thrown on the wards straight away, more or less. You also had to go on the ward from half past seven till nine, before you were sent to the classroom. To me, the conditions seemed dreadful. They weren't, of course, but you know, the only hospital I had really seen was a private nursing home in Ireland. I used to think, 'I wonder where Irish people go when they're sick. I'm sure none of them would want to come in here.' At the time it was a municipal hospital, run by the LCC for the masses. It was only in 1930 that they had taken over those places, which were workhouses, and converted them into LCC hospitals, as they called them in those days.

The work was very hard, but hard work didn't worry me because, as I told you, I'd had six years at home. No, I found the study very hard. I wasn't disciplined towards study. The majority had just left school and they were used to studying. We were called at half-past six, to breakfast at seven. At ten-past seven the big dining-room doors were shut, everybody was supposed to be in the dining-room then. Night sister said grace, and you all had to be there. You had your breakfast quickly, then back up to your room and leave it tidy, your bed made and everything. If you just pulled the clothes up and it wasn't all nice and flat, when you came off at break time your bed'd be stripped.

What I remember best of all is the sorting out of the laundry. You had a stack of laundry thrown out from the sluice, and the most junior nurse sorted all that out into its different piles. You had hand towels and bath towels, umpteen different kinds of towels – you'd use paper towels today. And umpteen different kinds of sheets – I thought there was only two kinds of sheets, but then there were a dozen of them. You had to make separate piles of all this and then, when it was all done, you told the sister and she came with the book and entered it. Then you counted it and bagged it. It was filthy, dirty linen of all kinds. Well, I didn't think this ever happened in real life at all you know! The other dreadful job was the sputum mugs. Every patient had a sputum mug and you had to collect all those after breakfast. The wards had about thirty, forty beds. Every patient wanted their own sputum mug back. There were no names, numbers or anything else on them, but they all wanted their own back! You had to empty them, put in a bit of disinfectant, wash them out in the sluice and put them back on the lockers. These two jobs you had to do before you went into the lecture room at ten. At half-past nine we went out for what we used to call lunch, nowadays it's coffee break, but in those days we called it lunch.

That first year we got £2 13s. 4d. a month, living in, of course. We got food and all the hot water in the world, because you were told you had to have a bath every day, otherwise you were going to go off with all kinds of diseases. The preliminary training was a great time because you had a half day on Saturday and then Sunday off. Well, of course, after your four weeks in there, that finished. You were a nurse then! You had one day off a week, and we used to finish two evenings at five, or was it half past five. Or you were off in the afternoon. Now this is where we Irish girls used to get into trouble, because we never had 'afternoons' in Ireland, we only had 'evenings'. The staff nurse would say to you in the morning when she was arranging who goes to what meal, 'What time are you off today?' I'd say 'evening', and she'd have the duty list in her hand and say, 'You're *not*, you're off in the afternoon.' Claiming an evening off when you weren't due was the biggest crime. Oh, the telling off I got from her! She thought I was trying to cheat, that I wanted an evening off when I was off two to four, in other words. I soon learnt to say afternoon! There were lots of language problems like that.

When the NHS came in, after the war, it didn't make a big difference. It was a very slow process. About the only thing you noticed at first was that your supplies were coming from a different quarter. The doctors of course did their damndest to stop it. It was a saying going round the hospitals at that time, that it had to be a very bad emergency to find a doctor, because they were continuously at meetings trying to oppose it.

The war was on at this time, and Ireland was neutral. That affected us in some ways. But we were looked after, it was a sheltered life living in a nurses' home, very sheltered. We weren't exposed to so much prejudice – not in the same ways as somebody who's walking the streets looking for a room. We didn't have to live with a household like the chaps living in digs did. Although Irish people were treated as aliens during the war. We had to report to the police every three months, we were on emergency tickets all the time. There were passports at the time – they didn't call them passports – but we had to get a visa to go home on holidays. Nothing will ever replace that first holiday ... the anticipation of that first holiday. And a whole day was wasted, waiting for that visa, when you could have been going. You had to save up, the fare cost quite a lot then. We got twenty-one days' holidays then, back in '43, and an awful lot of people weren't getting any paid holidays at that time. We Irish were allowed to take that all together. It was put up in the dining room, you'd go and see your name on there for three weeks' holiday from so and so date, you know.

It was never a lonely life, because we were always a crowd. We went to the Irish dances all over London. I met my husband in a dance hall. We went back to Ireland to be married – by my cousin, the priest. He was pleased. We lived down at the Angel at first, and we had two children – two girls. Later on we moved to Ilford.

We weren't too conscious at all of being Irish at that time. There was no terrorism in those days. Maybe there were little bits of prejudice, but we took it in good part. The Irish joke was always around. You always told jokes about the Englishman, the Scotsman and the Irishman, didn't you? It's not about the Englishman, the Irishman and the Scotsman anymore, it's just the Irishman, isn't it? I think they are pretty cruel today. I think the problems in Northern Ireland have changed the whole situation. When a bombing or anything like that happens I say, 'Thank God for supermarkets', because you don't have to speak, you don't have to ask for a loaf of bread. I do feel intimidated. I wouldn't want to get into a difficult situation, because I wouldn't know how I'd react. When I buy *The Irish Post* I fold it over when I am in the shop – and I like to buy it in an Indian shop. I notice myself doing all these things, very much so.

The English don't try to understand Irish people. But then they've learnt nothing. They don't realise that they have lived in so many countries and they have only tried to wipe out the ways of the people there, and stamp their way on the country. They are a very lonely people among themselves, they have no culture.

I suppose in the main I would say that nine out of ten Irish people that have come here have more or less the same story. Came, worked, married, brought up a family, and you did it, you didn't ask too much. The Irish back home certainly never knew how you did it. From your own generation, y'know, your brothers and sisters, you didn't have any sympathy. They didn't understand it. They didn't see the sacrifice you made in getting children home to Ireland every year to see their grandparents, to make them a part of things. I mean, I only had two children, some people had four and five children. They didn't put themselves in our place, what it cost to take them, looking immaculate, new clothes, all the rest, and to have enough money in your pocket to spend. I think those of us that left in the forties and fifties made it possible for them at home to have what they have today. After all, if we had all stayed there it would all have to be chopped up a little bit more, wouldn't it? We made room, and made it possible.

Nancy returned to live in Ireland last year.

A Traveller in England

'There's a byelaw to say you must be on your way
And another to say you can't wander'

Nellie Power is one of an estimated 15,000 Irish travellers in Britain. She describes the changes in their way of life, and the differences between her life and her mother's.

I never travelled 'till after I got married. I identified with travellers, I knew that I was one of them – I just took it for granted – but to be honest, I didn't really think that I'd ever go travelling. I lived with my grandparents when I was young, with my four sisters and one brother. They had a house in Athlone, because that's where they originally came from and I was born there in 1951. My mother and father were travelling. They used to travel around with the barrel-top wagons and mend buckets and kettles, stuff like that – what you call tinsmen. My mother used to go begging, and my father would make these buckets and things, and she'd sell them.

In Athlone there's an awful lot of travellers, at least a hundred families of travellers settled in houses. Those families grow up and they'll settle into houses again, and maybe there's about one in each family'll go travelling. My mother came over here when I was about eight, but my gran and grandfather wouldn't let me come. They didn't want me to travel. It never really dawned on me that I would travel, but the way it is for my kids today, none of them wants to move into a house, they just want to stay in a caravan. My eldest girl is getting married, and her and her boy, they're off on the road.

I went to an all-girls' school in Athlone. I found the nuns very hard, very strict – especially when they got that cane out! I often went home with blisters out on my hands as big as plums. I was glad when I left. Some travelling children refused to come into school, they used to get an awful lot of abuse, and were called names, called dirty and one thing and another. I felt sorry for them because I knew what kind of a life they had. My own uncles and their kids were on the road, and I used to go out visiting them, and I'd see how hard it was. They might have to go about two miles down the road for a bucket of water, and maybe in the morning it'd be raining, and they'd have no way of cooking with the sticks probably soaking wet. At least now you can buy a bottle of gas, and you can do your cooking inside. The travellers years ago really had it tough.

I finished school at fourteen, and got a job in a laundry. That was run by nuns too! They were all young girls working there, just out of school. A lot of girls used to come from a home in Moate to work for the nuns, and they'd sleep there as well, so it was really harder for them than it was for us, because we could go home, you know.

I worked on a presser, in an ironing room. There were seven girls doing the ironing, and I had to keep them going. I'd press the back of the shirts and the fronts of them and the sleeves, and they'd do the cuffs and the collars. I had to keep seven girls going with one presser. It was from nine o'clock in the morning till seven o'clock in the evening, and we got paid £1.50 a week. By the time I left I was only earning £3, so it was really hard. I was sixteen and a half then.

Myself and two friends wrote to an agency and we got a job over here in Guildford. More nuns – running a big college where all these blokes were training to be priests. We were cleaning rooms, washing up, and one thing and another. We were the only three Irish girls. There were some girls from Yugoslavia and Switzerland, and we were trying to teach them some English, what the words meant, you know. But it was very lonely – terribly lonely altogether. One of my friends left, she packed it in and went home. My other friend got engaged and ended up marrying and going back to live in Ireland, so I was left on my own.

While I was in Guildford, Johnny came to see me. I'd known him since I was about seven, because my uncle married his sister and when his family came over to live in Manchester, he used to come back every year for a holiday. He started coming to see me, and that was it! I went down to Manchester with him, and we were married there. My mother and father came across for the wedding. We lived in Manchester about two or three years until I had Norah. We used to get rented rooms – we never had any problems. I think the way it is with Manchester people, they're more used to the travellers than people in London are. For centuries there's been travellers in Manchester, and they get to know the people, and the people are good to them.

We started travelling in 1977. We were living in a prefab in Mile End, and a lot of my husband's relations came up to London, and they were all in caravans. We decided then to move around. It was a bit difficult at first, getting used to a smaller space and things like that, but we got used to it. It's difficult finding places to stop now, and we get a lot of hassle from the police. The men will all go looking for a camp, they just see an open space and try to get in and get as long as they can out of it. If it's council ground it's not too bad, you know, you'll get a good few weeks out of it, but if it's private, they can take you to court within a week and you're out. Say, for instance now, we were getting evicted from here, we'd have to go out and tidy up a place before we'd move in, and when we got evicted just move straight there.

When we moved in here the trees were really high, right the way over the whole place. We had to clear the lot out. The council told us that we could move in, but they couldn't give us official permission. When we were moving the police came and hooked the trailer up to a van and towed us half way up the street. I had the baby lying in the bed there, and the gas fire on. I told them, but they just rocked the whole trailer from side to side, throwing the child around in the bed, and the fire on. They told us that we'd no right to be in here. About two weeks later we came back again, about five o'clock in the morning, and brought the trailer down. The police came again, but I gave them the council's number and said they knew I had permission.

A couple of weeks after, they came back again at night, saying they'd had a report of stolen churns. I had two churns out at the front of the trailer, which we'd had for about five or six years. We weren't even using them, because we had running water here, you know. They came in and wanted to know where we got the churns from. My husband was arrested, my sister-in-law was arrested and my daughter was arrested, all over these old churns. Two of them got hold of my daughter – she was sixteen at the time – one took her by the legs and the other just took her by her hair, and threw her right against the back of the police van. They were kept overnight and in the police station they said to them, 'We've got a lovely surprise for you in here, we've got a gas chamber for all the travellers, and all the blacks.' Next morning they went to court and were bound over to keep the peace.

Another time, my door just opens up and in steps a policeman wanting to know how many boys we have, and what ages they are. I asked him, 'What do you want to know all this for, what does it matter?' 'Because one of these boys jumped over that wall and started to break into a house over there,' he said. I asked him how old the boy was. 'He was about sixteen or seventeen.' 'My two boys, there they are,' I said, 'one is three and the other is six.' He just looked and said, 'Behave yourselves, and we won't have to be caught up with you.' They're definitely against the travellers. I mean, it would be different if you were doing something.

When we're moving camp, the woman is never brought to see what she's moving into beforehand. The muck could be up to your knees, but the men don't think about that. A woman's got the worry of everything really. In a mucky camp, you get the kids coming in with muck up to their knees and you've got to try and keep the place clean. Generally, it's the same thing every

179

day – keeping the place clean. When I was in a house, I found that when you'd cleaned your house, your house is clean, and if you're using the kitchen, it's only the kitchen that's getting dirty. In a trailer, no matter how many times a day you clean up, all you've got to do is get one meal ready, and you've got to go back over the whole lot again. It's not too bad in the summertime, but in the wintertime it's really tough. Hot water is a very hard problem. You've only got the cold water and you've got to boil kettles or buckets of water when you need it. In the wintertime you can find that your gas bottle is freezing up, and you can be without gas until that thaws out. And you've got to do your shopping whether it's raining, snowing – you've got no fridges to keep food in for a few days – it's a daily thing. And washing clothes – it's OK if you just want to wash out something, but what I do, I send all my clothes over to the big wash-house twice a week. I just send the kids to do it. It's not too expensive over there, it's 80p for a machine, and you can use the roller if you want, so it's not too bad. Going to the launderette cost me £7 the week before last, for two machines – I couldn't afford to do that every week.

The council don't provide any sites at all, not in Camden. The only responsibility that they'll take is to provide portable toilets, and maybe they'll bring a tank of water. But they rent the toilets off some firm, and they are useless, because they won't come and empty them. You'll be phoning them up for weeks and weeks to come and empty it. When we moved in here, my husband found a water pipe, and we managed to get a flush toilet because we had the water – but it was just down to us that we found the water. Where we were before, we had to collect water every day from a garage in the big churns.

Some other boroughs provide sites, but to be honest I can't really leave the area on account of the kids going to school. If I leave that's the end of their education, and that is important, because travelling kids don't really get that much of a chance in life. If we moved and I put them into a new school, they're going to be bullied and called names, which we did have when they started here. There was one really, really nasty little boy – he was out on his own. He'd throw stones and call names, and his mother and father didn't want to know. Martin came back from school with the whole print of this young lad's foot on his back. I went round and I told the teacher that I was taking the kids out of school. 'I can't have him coming to school if the kids are going to beat him up.' She was really good about it. She got in touch with his parents and told them, while I was there, that if he didn't stop she was going to expel him. Since then, that family have left, and everything has quietened down. The other kids now want mine to go out and play with them, you know, they're mixing in well and they're not being called names like 'gypsies' or 'tinkers' or anything. I've always told them if anybody calls them names like 'You're a traveller', or 'You're a tinker', they should say, 'Yes, I am, I know I am. I'm proud of it.'

Really and truly, most of the Irish people over here are more against the

Nellie Power

travellers than English people are. I've never been to the Irish Centre for a drink, because a lot of travellers are barred, so we don't bother going up there. I think what it is, they're ashamed of travellers. It really hurts to describe. I think of myself as Irish. My five children were born in England, yet they call themselves Irish travellers. That's what they say, 'Irish travellers'. But when people know that you're a traveller, they don't think of you as Irish, they just say you're a traveller. A lot of pubs put up a sign that says 'No Travellers' – that means that even though you've never been in the pub, just because you're a traveller you can't go in them. It gets you when you're walking along the street and you look and see that written there. You're written off just because you're a traveller. You just can't win.

I know people who have had problems being registered with a doctor. My husband's nephew took their little baby, eight or nine weeks old, to the doctor, and he said, 'I don't want nothing to do with you – go to the hospital if you want to. I'm not seeing you.' A lot of doctors are like that. Even my brother-in-law, who's a diabetic, couldn't get a doctor to register him. I'm lucky really, because the doctor I have used to visit a camp we were staying at, and we've been with him ever since. He used to come out to the site when he didn't really have to bother, and spend an hour, just to see that everything was OK.

Things have changed a lot for travellers over the years. It makes me very sad. Things like storytelling and campfires – over here you can't light a fire, because they send for the police or the fire brigade. I think it's mostly the older generation that'd tell you stories about the banshees and things like that – though I don't know if I really believe in them. Television has taken over. If storytelling does die out, all those stories will be gone. Travellers still go to the fairs – there's a horse fair near Scotland – and to Epsom, to the Derby. A lot of travellers go home to Ballinasloe in October for the fair. I think that one is really more popular than the ones over here. Weddings are mostly a big do, especially if it's the first one that's getting married in the family. What happens is the mother and the father of both sides, they help pay for everything apart from the wedding cake and the bridal stuff. The mother of the girl will pay for that. We don't send out invitations, but everybody turns up. Even travellers you don't know, they'll turn up at a wedding! Hundreds of people come. The hardest part is getting the hall. My eldest is getting married – it's going to be an awful lot of hard work!

A travelling woman's life is very different to what it used to be. Women would buy little charms, clothes pegs, stuff like that and go round and sell them. The men would have a trade, and the women would sell the stuff and go begging as well, to feed the kids. There really isn't any of that left, there's no profit to be made out of it anyway. My grandmother, she used to go begging, and we'd often see her coming back and maybe she'd been away all day and she might have nothing, you know. You might starve for that day, so it was really tough. Things like the dole and social security have helped an awful lot. It isn't much, but it's made a big difference to our way of life.

182

Travellers are a very close community – you'll see the women up and down to the shops together, to the market, and the kids always playing together. We know where everybody is, or we could easily find out. That can be a bad thing, if you don't want to be found, but it also means that you've got the support at the back of you and we do need it. Older people now, they're never put into a home, or anything like that. They'll have their own independence, a caravan of their own, but they'll always move with the sons or the daughters, or whoever they're with, they'll stay in the one camp with them. Single women stay with their families too. If a marriage breaks up, the man will go his way and the woman will go her way, and that's it. Probably what would happen is you'd go home and stay with your own people. It would be really tough to be on your own in a caravan, because you've got kids and you've got to get water and gas and stuff like that, and most women don't know how to drive. You'd probably have your own trailer, but with your own people, and then anything that's needed the brother or whoever's there would help out.

People think the travellers are just here today and they want to be gone tomorrow; it's not going to be like that you know. Travellers are here, and the majority of women around my age, all their kids were born in this country. They grow up and marry into other travelling families, they're not just going to disappear. I think myself maybe travellers should get together and start fighting for themselves. It would be a start. It happened in Dublin, it really opened up their eyes back there when the travellers started marching. That's what we should do over here, take a convoy of trailers down to Downing Street or park them at Buckingham Palace. But you can't live the life that you want to live, you know. I went and put my name down for a house the other day, because I can't see no future in this. It would be different if you had a site or something, or even if you could travel. But there's nowhere you can travel, is there? And it's getting worse as the years go on.

A Seventies Emigrant

Moving outwards

Tricia Darragh is one of a younger generation of women who left Ireland in the mid-seventies. Here, she describes some of the choices she has made in her life, and her decision to eventually return to Ireland.

I came to London when I was twenty-one. I think maybe I had vague notions about becoming a social worker, and it seemed a lot easier to do that sort of thing here. So I came over and stayed with an auntie. My mother rang and said, 'Tricia's coming over, look after her.' I stayed with her for a while, while I found a job and a place to live. I found that time quite difficult, because I was very much in an Irish community, you know, round Kilburn, Willesden, and I just didn't want to have anything to do with it. It was like I was rejecting everything about it. I quickly got myself a job in Kensington High Street and a flat in West Ken., and sort of broke all connections with anybody Irish for a long time.

I had felt quite stifled in Ireland, and very isolated. I was the first of five children, and the first one in my family ever to go to secondary school. I think I was there a year when free education was introduced. I was really 'good' in primary school. In fact, I can remember winning a prize for not missing a day in the whole year – you know, things like that. I stopped being a good little girl very quickly when I went to secondary school. I started being rebellious and not being interested in a lot of what was offered and wanting other things.

I really wanted to do economics, and they didn't provide that as an option at our school. So I suggested, very reasonably I thought, that I could take a free period, and do economics in the technical school in the evening. They thought that was the extreme in rebelliousness, and why couldn't I just be a good little girl and accept what was provided. I started being very difficult in religious classes. I remember once in a religious exam I just wrote basically what I believed. One of the nuns brought it back into the room and trying to be nice to me, she said, 'You probably didn't realise, but a lot of what you wrote in here is heresy, so, I'd like you to just change it before we send it to the Archbishop.' I refused to change it. Eventually I was told that they weren't really happy to have me in the school!

I often used to go down to Rathmines library, instead of going to school, and sit and read things I was interested in. I was very interested in communism, for instance. I mean, you just weren't allowed to talk about that. In the end I left school and went to work with the Simon Community.[1] My parents found this really difficult, because neither of them had really had the opportunity to have an education. My father in particular put all his hopes on me, and he was just shattered when I had these opportunities and rejected them.

When I was about eighteen I got very involved with a man I met through the Simon Community, and we took off on our travels around Ireland. I remember setting off one January and travelling round till March. We travelled by hitching, and quite often we'd knock on a door and ask if we could sleep in the haybarn, and sometimes we'd be met with a shotgun and other times we'd be invited in for breakfast the next morning; you know, really different reactions. There were never any awkward questions about a young girl travelling around with a man!

Then I got pregnant, and had a baby who was adopted. I didn't actually admit it to myself until I was about five months pregnant and I never told the father of the child. He had a lot of problems, was manic depressive and had spent a lot of his life in prison. I knew it wasn't a situation that I wanted to get into, being dependent on him, and having a child. I left Dublin and went to live with a family who were involved in a group called Ally.[2]

My family were very good to me when I was pregnant. I can remember strange things, like my father coming to see me and taking me out for a drink. He was obviously really uncomfortable and embrarrassed at the situation, but doing his best; not talking about it really. They were as good as they could be at the time, you know. I had to be hidden away in the country because nobody could possibly know about it ... 'What would the neighbours say?' and that whole thing.

She was six days old when she was taken away, and I was still in hospital. It was incredibly difficult. At the same time, I just didn't see any choice. They didn't even have unmarried mothers' allowance in those days. I had quite strong ideas about what a child needed and I just didn't see any way that I could possibly do it on my own. I don't know now ... I can't remember clearly how much it was what other people would say, but I just thought it would be better for the child. I've been through a lot of pain with the adoption that I've just kept inside me. It's only in recent years that I've been able to talk about it.

After that I went back to Dublin and lived at home for a while. I was making big changes in my life then. There were more and more ways that I felt like I was a freak, that I didn't fit in, that I was having these feelings and ideas that I couldn't share with anybody. I became a vegetarian, which was a really big thing for me. I didn't want to live the way the people around me were living, you know. So it wasn't primarily that I was desperate for work that I left, or any of the traditional reasons for leaving.

I was really fascinated meeting people from other places when I came to London first. I can remember being on a high from that for a long time – just getting on buses and tubes and wanting to go to people and ask them, you know, where they were from. It seemed an alternative to travelling – I could meet people from all over the world here. And I did to some extent. I remember getting a job where I had to have two references and the woman in the job asked me, 'Have you not got any English friends?' one of the referees was Malaysian and the other was Indian – and me saying quite proudly, 'No, I haven't!' I met Zaini's father when he was coming out of an exam and we literally just started talking to each other. For a long time we just had a casual friendship and I met a lot of his friends who were foreign students. Most of the people I met in London were not from this culture, hadn't actually had the experience of growing up here.

I worked as an interviewer in an employment agency for a good while, and that was an education. I mean, I really got to know English racism when I was there. I was quite shocked, for instance, there were certain jobs that they didn't send black people for. You know, there was this silent agreement amongst them. So I got into a lot of arguments with them, and I left on quite bad terms in the end.

I was very interested in alternative education, so got a little bit involved in a free school which was the far side of Shepherd's Bush. I came in contact with a group in Hammersmith who were setting up a nursery and I was the first paid worker there, working with two to five year olds.

I got pregnant with Zaini very soon after I started working there. For some reason I was ecstatically happy about it. It wasn't a rational thing. I knew there were a whole lot of questions. I knew, for instance, that I wasn't in love with his father. He'd finished his studies and was going back to Malaysia, which I was quite glad about. I knew that there would possibly be difficulties with a child of mixed race, and I just didn't know where I was going to be living, or how I was going to be living. At the same time, no matter what the reasoning was, I felt incredibly well, and was kind of going round singing and dancing. It was at a time when I was beginning to meet women who were living quite strong independent lives, sometimes women who had children on their own, and I was beginning to think about the possibility of not having relationships with men – and I found myself pregnant! I'd begun to be attracted to women. So there was all that as well.

So, Hussain went back to Malaysia. He wanted me to go with him, and I wouldn't go. I stayed here and carried on working as long as I could. I visited my GP and the midwife regularly. I wasn't allowed to have the baby at home, so I went into what they call a GP unit, which meant that I'd only stay in there for forty-eight hours. I horrified my mother by walking there on the morning Zaini was born – she thought that was a ridiculous thing to do. It was only ten minutes away from where I lived, and I'd been awake all night in labour. So I got up at five or six o'clock in the morning and got the bag and went into hospital. My mother was really shocked afterwards when I told her what I'd done. But it was very easy, and I'm quite healthy anyway. He was a very easy child. What was quite striking was the approval I got after he was born. I can remember walking down the street that I lived in and lots of people saying

Tricia Darragh and Zaini

hello to me, who wouldn't have said hello to me a few months before. There's something about being a mother which brought this out in people. I was quite resentful of this approval. I thought, I've lived in this street for months, nobody's ever said hello to me, and now because I'm coming along with this baby they all want to have a look at the baby and say hello, you know. In fact, I was doing the right thing for once, I didn't like it at all – this approval!

When Zaini was ten weeks old I went to Malaysia to visit Hussain. I'd promised him before he went home that I would. When I got there I was persuaded to stay. I got married so that I could stay, and stayed a year and a half. I was really excited going to Malaysia, even before I came to London I had a great interest in other places, other cultures. One thing that struck me in Malaysia was that in the areas that hadn't been influenced by the British, there was a lot of poverty in the material sense, but they were culturally very rich. They had really held on to their arts and crafts. You'd see women on the east coast, out on the porches, making beautiful batiks, and the men made incredibly gorgeous kites, enormous and really intricately designed. They would make shadow puppets and have shadow plays and things. On the other hand, where they seemed more prosperous they were very much influenced by western ways, and they'd bring their children up on hamburgers and they'd shop in the supermarket. It confused me a lot at the time.

It's hard to talk very fairly about that time now, because I feel that it was a big mistake. At the time it was quite frightening to suddenly find myself alone with this child. I suppose what persuaded me to stay in Malaysia was that here was this other person offering to share that responsibility. I had women friends who would come and visit and be really helpful and supportive, but basically I was on my own, and that was a frightening responsibility. Also, Hussain, I think, felt really strongly about his son. He got really, really upset and said how can you bring my son to see me and take him away, and persuaded me to stay for six months. That was the initial agreement, that I would stay for six months and give it a fair try. I had a return ticket and I cashed it in, and he agreed to pay my fare in six months' time if I wasn't happy. But, of course, after six months he didn't agree at all and made it impossible for me to leave. It was a big turning point for me as far as relationships with men go. I think that was the hardest thing about that whole time, discovering that I was more important to him as a possession almost. Most of all I had thought he was my friend, you know.

I was unwilling for a long time to leave until he accepted it. I was working really hard at explaining to him why I needed to leave, believing he would eventually understand. But gradually I saw that he really didn't care whether I was happy or not. He actually became quite violent and threatened to kill us all, and we had some really horrific scenes, and I decided I just couldn't take it any more. My sister was saving up to visit me, and my friend, so I wrote to them both and said, 'Look, between you send me a ticket, quick.'

I made all the arrangements secretly – the thing that really confirmed my decision to leave was that he didn't notice. He didn't notice any change in me. I phoned him from the airport just as I was about to get on the plane to say that I was leaving and, of course, he cried and got very upset and said how could I do that to him, and please wait and talk about it, and all the rest. I was just very cold and hard and said goodbye, you know. I had a five hour wait in Bangkok Airport and that was really hard, expecting that he would arrive any minute with his brothers or whatever and that I just wouldn't have any say. But anyway, we got through it all and I got back here and lived with some friends, and for a while worried that he'd come after me and try to take Zaini, but he didn't.

It was a hard time, in Malaysia, but maybe it wasn't as hard as I would find it now, because I think I really didn't have a strong sense of myself at all, my own needs, or rights even. I think I had rejected a lot that had to do with being Irish, and I hadn't really got anything to replace it. I knew what I didn't want. I had this very strong sense of myself as being odd, because I wasn't content just to get married and have children and settle down. I knew I had needs beyond that. What I decided after my experience was that if I was ever to get involved with a man again, I would be very, very sure that we were really friends first. However, some eighteen months later I discovered that all my really close friends are women!

Growing up in Ireland, I can't remember ever having heard about lesbianism. I had no images whatever, good or bad. Despite my feelings of strength and independence, when it came to sex I basically went along with what men expected of me. It was something I don't think I felt I had any control over. The thing about getting pregnant for instance, not taking responsibility for my sexuality. If I made any decision at all, it was that I wouldn't sort out anything about contraceptives, so it was like allowing things to happen, not taking responsibility, which I think is very much connected with our lack of education to do with sex – not really knowing our own bodies, not taking any pleasure in our bodies, not knowing that women could have orgasms, not knowing that I had a clitoris until a man told me – it's crazy!

After a few months back in London I went back to work in the nursery and there were two lesbians working there. We talked a lot, and I can remember thinking, it's a pity I'm not a lesbian. I thought that because I'd had relationships with men and had children, that I wasn't. It took me a while to realise that I could actually choose to be, if I wanted to be, you know. That was a very powerful feeling. Here I was, maybe for the first time, making a real choice about my life, and so I didn't have that feeling that a lot of women seem to have had, of guilt, or trying to keep a secret, or really struggling within themselves. For me, it was a very positive, very good choice that I made. I didn't have any trouble telling people about it, or any of that. I mean, I told my mother quite soon, and basically I told pretty well anybody that I had anything to do with. I felt really good about it, you know.

My mother didn't believe it. She still doesn't believe it. She thinks it's a phase I'm going through because I had a bad time with men, you know. I just don't fit into whatever image she has of lesbians. On an emotional level she can totally understand. She has women friends she's really close to. I remember one of the first things she said when I told her was, 'Well, of course men and women can't be friends!'

The woman I got involved with, it was her first relationship with a woman as well. There wasn't any great passionate thing, which I think was really good for us in the end, because it was totally safe. We had months of going to bed together and giggling, and we'd talk about how we were used to somebody else making all the moves, and it was just the right way for both of us, you know.

At the same time, I was really coming into my strength as a woman around this time. I started doing a carpentry course, for instance, and that gave me an amazing sense of my own capabilities. I just felt that I could do whatever I chose to do. I was constantly meeting women who were doing similar things. So it wasn't just the coming out as a lesbian, there was getting involved in women's groups, trying to set up a local women's centre, the Women in Manual Trades group, and eventually there was the Lesbian Mothers group – there was lots happening, and I was pretty well in the thick of it.

As well as all this, slowly but surely I felt the need growing to be involved in an Irish women's group. It was a very slow process, I'd been through so many other things. Somehow I suppose being lesbian cut me off even further, you know, it increased that strength of separateness from other Irish people. I felt a great confusion over a long period and a need to talk with other Irish women before I actually did anything about it. And I found that when I began to do that it caused problems with the women I was close to. They saw it as being divisive, irrelevant – you know, 'Oh, we're all women, after all.' Then I saw an ad. in the bookshop, Sisterwrite, about an Irish women's group, so I immediately rang up. We met a few times and started putting ads around and started an Irish women's group. I think that was the first, certainly the first that any of us knew of.

It hasn't always been that easy. I've had moments of real despair. It seemed like my home was in the women's movement, that at last I'd found a place where I could be me, and find others who I could identify with. But there was the antagonism of some women who just didn't want to know me, because I had a boy. So there were some difficult times justifying to myself, as well as to other women, the time and energy and the effort that I was putting into raising this young man. There were feelings and pressures coming from inside me, or outside, I really don't know, that I was going to have to choose between my son and women. That was very painful for a while. But what I decided was that I didn't have any reason, coming from him personally, to dislike him in any way, and that I was going to carry on being his mother to the best of my abilities until such time as that would arise. I think that's the only way to do it. We live really well together, basically we like and respect each other. Of course there are things about him that I don't like and things about me that he doesn't like – he thinks that I'm really old-fashioned for instance! But there's no point about getting in a state about what he might be like when he's twenty. I'm really grateful that he's such a nice person now. You know, when he was five I thought they'll just undo it all when he goes to school. We had a lesbian mothers of sons group for a while, which was really helpful. There was a woman in that who had a daughter, as well as sons, who was able to say it's not because they're male that they're demanding. She was able to tell us really clearly that her daughter was just as stroppy or whatever it might be that we were having problems with. That was really reassuring to know, that any child was going to make such demands of me.

When Zaini was six we went back to live in Ireland. I'd known for quite a while that I wanted to go back and live in Ireland. At first, I felt like I didn't want to live in a city any more, or not such a big city anyway. I considered going to live in Sheffield, but I realised during that time that really what I wanted was to go home. Then my father died and that really made me want to go home much more quickly. I wanted to be closer to my mother, so I applied for a place in Coleraine university. It's that bit nearer Dublin, I could see my mother more regularly and just start making contacts in Ireland, and you know, find ways to live there. I lived there for two years. I went to university for two terms. It was absolutely awful, but there was lots that was very important for me to learn I think, living in the North. We went in July. For me this was a big thing. This was going home, going back to Ireland. We arrived in Castlerock and they had all their Union Jacks out for the 12th of July! I thought, my God, where am I! That was quite a shock. I learned that you can't just dismiss the loyalist population as I might have in moments of anger in the past. I still haven't worked out any solution, but I just feel that I can think about the whole thing in a much more realistic way. It was strange being in the North, realising the distinctions that there obviously are between the North and the rest of Ireland. I was making really frequent trips down to Dublin and to Donegal and trying all the time to see Ireland as a whole, but it wasn't very easy in practice.

Zaini was very happy there. I chose to send him to a catholic school when we lived in the North, because the only choice was between catholic and protestant schools and so for cultural and political reasons I felt that before I even saw the schools that I would rather him go to the catholic school. At least there'd be some recognition of being in Ireland and being Irish, whereas in the protestant schools they have the British education system and that's it. We went to visit the schools. They were really official and business-like in the protestant school. The catholic school was further away, it was up in the hills where the catholic people lived, in the very poor land. It was a tiny, two-roomed school, two teachers, twenty-four children in the whole school, and it was a lovely, lovely school. I made it clear from the beginning that I didn't want him to have religious education, and they were fine about that.

Living in Ireland was important for Zaini as well. Because he has lived in Ireland and spent so much time around my family, he has a very strong sense of being Irish. I can't do the same on the Malay side. I tell him little bits of the language that I remember, and any books that I come across to do with Malaysia, he has them. I would like him to know more Malaysian people. I was very glad when he met a woman from Penang, where we used to live, at a friend's house. He was so excited about meeting her, seeing photographs of her family and thinking that one young child looked like him. It was so nice to see him making those connections and identifying in that way. I used to think I'd love to bring him back there. I used to plan, when he's about eleven I'll bring him back. I think I felt guilty about having taken him away from there, and responsible to take him back. But there's no way I could afford it now. Now I'm sure he'll go himself some day, and I would really encourage him to go.

My mother was very worried about me having a child of mixed race and the confusions that would cause for the child later on, but when he was actually on the scene he was just so lovely that the family were all mad about him. There was a bit of that sort of stuff – 'Oh, you'd hardly know', he looks so like me. And a lot of polite things – 'Oh you'd think he only had a suntan!' I haven't encountered as much racism with Zaini as I'd been aware of, for instance, when I'd worked with black children in London. Some people think there's something more acceptable about being oriental. It's seen as kind of exotic.

I have a black cousin in Dublin, and she's had a very hard time growing up there. She went through a time of feeling that she didn't like black people, and had to change school quite a few times because of name-calling and being subjected to nastiness. Recently she seems to feel a lot better about herself. Zaini had some quite overt hostility in Dublin a few years ago. I think he was about seven at the time and it was quite a big occasion for him because for the first time he was going to the shops on his own. It involved crossing two little roads and he was feeling quite proud of himself. He came back in tears, because these boys had thrown stones at him and called him blackie. He was hurt and he was angry, and he said, 'If this is what it's like in Ireland, I don't want to live here.' It was only the one incident, but it was very nasty.

I have a real sense of hope about living at home. There's something about the size of the place and the numbers of people that excites me, about how change can happen. The impact of something like the 'Late, Late Show',[3] for instance, fascinates me – you know, that ideas can spread very quickly and that tomorrow after Mass, everybody's talking about them. I don't think there's going to be any revolutionary change immediately, but there's something about that smallness and the facility with which ideas spread that you just don't have in England.

One of the *very* special things for me, that I want to mention, is that three years ago, just after I'd gone to live at home, there was a lesbian conference in Dublin. That was a really overwhelming experience for me, just to go there and to be surrounded by all these women who were Irish lesbians. It has made me feel very good about living at home.

Notes

1. A voluntary group which organises night shelters and soup runs for people sleeping rough.
2. A catholic voluntary organisation offering to help single women have their babies rather than have an abortion.
3. A very popular live television chat show on Saturday nights.

Work with Irish Prisoners

If they come in the morning ...

Sister Sarah Clarke was born in Co. Galway. She joined the Order of La Sainte Union in 1939 and subsequently trained as a teacher. She taught art and was headmistress of a school in Athlone. In 1957 she was transferred to work in England. She taught for a number of years and during the 1960s went to Chelsea Art College to study graphics. Here she reflects on the turn her life took in the early seventies.

I have a great devotion to the Stations of the Cross and I see the whole history of our people in the Stations, and especially in the Passion of Christ. How many trials have I stood at with families and I can always see Christ standing down there in the dock. How many times have I seen them starting and falling and getting into trouble and rising again. I have stood with their mothers as they met their sons after the cross. I have seen the people forced to help them – like the prison officers and probation officers, who are the Simians; and then the Veronicas, and the people like myself, who'll send them an odd card or do something.

Then we have the people who'll sit at television, the women of Jerusalem, and they are the tut-tutters, who really are sad, but don't do anything. The strip-searching – I never knew what strip-searching was. I thought it was just the taking off of clothes, but there's a lot more to it than that. It's the depersonalising of people. Then we have the people in the Irish Embassy who say 'Oh well, they should say they're sorry.' Dismas never said he was sorry. Dismas spoke the truth. Then, of course, the awful plight of what I call the burial – the burial in prison and the burial of the family. For the families it's a kind of perpetual bereavement.

Looking back over my life, I realise that being voiceless and marginalised myself in a religious community for many years prepared me for work with voiceless and marginalised prisoners and their families. In the early days, I was naive in that I thought that people were good – that everyone was good and that somehow if they knew the right thing, they would act justly. The word 'politics' was no part of my thinking. In 1969, when Belfast was burning, I went to Reverend Mother in the convent here and said that we should do something else as well as praying for the sufferings of the people of Northern Ireland. She sent me to the community confessor who suggested that I join the Northern Ireland Civil Rights Association [NICRA]. I had never heard of them. I attended my first meeting and there was quite a lot of surprise at a nun joining. I don't think I was welcome at first, but eventually I was fully accepted. I learnt many things quickly – things that we were unaware of in the sheltered life of a convent. I learned that the police weren't always right. 'Oh, the police wouldn't do that,' I would say at the meetings, and a look of unbelieving would go around the table, as much as to say, 'What kind of innocent is she?' There was always a friend present, however, who would say, 'I'll tell you afterwards,' and who brought me up to date. I was being educated very fast. Little did I think then, that I was being prepared to deal with the Prevention of Terrorism Act and all its atrocities.

By that time, Vatican II had come and it made things easier for us nuns. Pope John XXIII declared the supremacy of one's conscience and with this came the right of nuns to speak as well as listen to their superiors. We started talking in the refectory – it was an opening up of the way of life. At this time, civil rights marches began, American nuns were out protesting and I was organising some here. My superiors were happiest, however, when I was working behind the scenes, which I mainly did. But there were times when I felt guilty for not being out protesting, when others more vulnerable were sticking their necks out on our behalf, risking having their names put on police files.

To my surprise then, I was elected secretary of the executive committee of NICRA, London. Only three or four people turned up for the first meeting after my election and I thought they had all stayed away because of me being a nun. But one by one, they rang in to say that they had been raided by the police. It was after the Aldershot bombing. I dashed home from the meeting to see if they had raided the convent. It was late and everything was quiet, so I went to Reverend Mother's door to find out if the police had been. She said, 'What would they come here for . . . and even if they had come, what harm? You have nothing to be afraid of.' That was reassuring. Circumstances forced me to leave NICRA, but the apprenticeship I served there helped me to readjust my outlook and to view events through the eyes of the poor and oppressed.

At the end of 1974, the PTA was passed. I didn't know what the PTA was, or even that it had become law! My MP warned me to be careful. I wasn't doing anything, but you didn't have to be doing anything – to be Irish was enough to get you into trouble. To help the ordinary Irish man or woman in trouble was dangerous. There were widespread arrests – hundreds of Irish people were picked up, including the Birmingham Six, the Guildford Four, the Maguire Family[1] and Guiseppe Conlon R.I.P.,[2] and for the first time I experienced the PTA in all its horrors. People picked up under the PTA had no rights whatsoever in those early days. They disappeared. Eventually, we found out that they could be held for seven days. Police denied that they were holding people. Detainees were questioned at all hours, day and night, and solicitors were not allowed in. It was a very anxious time for the families of those detained. Many of the families turned to Fathers Faul, Murray and Brady and they, in turn, asked me to help. My work with prisoners began. We were involved with those cases, right from the start, and realised what was happening.

We had several cases each week. At that time, I was teaching and doing typography research, so the nights were spent on the phone to police stations around the country and to solicitors. I built up a file of solicitors near ports, airports and in all the main cities and, of course, the families were kept informed of what I was doing. My phone bill was colossal. I had no money to pay the bills. I often prayed for someone to give me a present and I'd get one – which shows me that it's the hand of God. Providence always provided. Then, because of eye trouble, I had to give up all my other work so I could work full-time with the prisoners and their families. Up until 1975 there was no shortage of helpers, people were vying with one another to help – bringing parcels to the prisons, going to the airport or to the court. But such people became suspect; their homes were raided, their families terrorised and many lost their jobs because of the PTA and had to go back to Ireland. Others became too frightened to help any more. Gradually, everyone was gone.

It was terrible from 1975 to 1981. That was the worst period; I call it the 'bad time'. Police with dogs, guns and vans swooped on houses in the early hours of the morning, frightening young children, damaging property and making innocent law-abiding citizens targets of suspicion in their streets and neighbourhoods. If they were anyway involved, and when I say 'involved', I mean anyway Irish at all, they were raided or taken in. After these raids, the families were stunned and isolated. It was heart-rending to see their gratitude and relief when a nun visited them. I was very frightened as well and sometimes wondered if I was taken in, would anyone visit me? If I hadn't been a nun, I would have been arrested too.

It frightened me to see what a few days in a police station could do to people. I have seen very strong women and men, who I thought nothing would frighten, come out like jelly. The conditions in which women and children were held were dreadful. They refused women sanitary towels, held them for seven days without policewomen present, refused them medicines,

Sister Sarah Clarke

clean blankets or washing facilities – it was appalling. Young children were questioned about their fathers' and mothers' habits and friends, and they were bribed with sweets for information. In at least one instance, young children were kept all night in a police station, questioned for long hours and left to sleep on a window-ledge. Their mother had gone to the police station to report her husband missing and they came and arrested her and all her family.

These were very bad times and for years, the Irish people took all this hardship lying down. Family after family refused to allow me to publish the damage done to them and their property, out of genuine fear of retaliation. If what happened here happened in Russia, the whole world would be up in arms, but because it has happened in Britain, and we have this so-called fair play and justice, nobody wants to know. It doesn't happen to me, therefore, it doesn't happen; and if it does happen to people, they must be guilty! The greatest cause of sorrow to me was the indifference and lack of support from our own well-off powerful Irish brothers and sisters who, when they learnt that I was working for Irish prisoners, fled from me as from a plague. No country in the world would abandon its people as the Irish government has done for so long. Having appealed to successive Irish governments since 1970 on behalf of prisoners and their families, one sees that they don't want to know anything about our own people in trouble – apparent failures. They want to know you if you're a success, but if you're not, they don't want to know. I think the Irish people are a bit like that too; we don't see the value of failure. Failure brings out the best in you. By worldly standards, Christ dying on the gibbet was a failure.

At the moment, there's about fifty Irish political prisoners in jail here, a few women, but mainly men and nearly all of these are doing life sentences. It would normally be about ten years, but because they're Irish prisoners, they'll often do life. The most difficult problem they're facing now is isolation as they are often isolated even in different wings of the same jail. This is justified in the name of legitimate defence and security of society, but the security in question is the security of the powerful. The families also suffer great hostilities. Every few weeks I meet them bringing their children with them on exhausting journeys to the remotest parts of Britain, trying to keep the father's memory alive in the family, when prison rules allow and common decency dictates that prisoners be held nearer their homes. One woman who has to fly all the way over from the North, gets a fifteen minute visit and she has to wait until the next day to get fifteen minutes more. The prisoners from the South of Ireland are in a very bad way. Their families often find it difficult because the Irish State doesn't give help to needy families to visit.

The wives of the prisoners have the full responsibility for the family, but get no sympathy. If they had a bereavement they'd have the Church and State putting their arms around them. They're not free to marry again, so for half a lifetime they remain faithful to their husbands. They have to pay the bills,

A prisoner waving through the bars of Brixton Gaol

raise the children, and they're not helped to carry this burden by having, on top of all that, to perpetually pinch and save to visit their loved ones.

My work is with the prisoners' families. I meet them on arrival, house them and drive them to the prison. I take weekly parcels to the prisoners for them and also write to the prisoners I've been in contact with down the years. Unfortunately, I'm not allowed in to visit them. Otherwise, I haven't experienced any direct harassment and being a nun has enabled me to continue with my work, even during the bad time.

The more I read the Gospel, the more I see that this is our concern. If we don't do it, who's going to do it? In seventeen years, the power of the Church has done little to help these prisoners to get moved nearer home. One senior chaplain said to me that it was policy to make the prisoners' loved ones suffer also, and he seemed to agree with such a policy. During his life, Christ never condemned the poor or oppressed but it seems to me that the Church is perpetually condemning them, unlike Christ. Surely we Christians believe Christ when he said, 'As long as you did it to one of my brethren, you did it to me?'

Notes

1. People convicted of bombing offences, all of whom have protested their innocence. All received lengthy sentences and campaigns have been mounted to clear their names.
2. Guiseppe Conlon, visiting the Maguires at the time of their arrest, was sentenced with them and died in prison.

Arriving in the Eighties

Other people's worlds

In the 1980s the high level of emigration from Ireland has more than equalled that of the 1950s. Rachel Harbron left Dublin in 1986 and here she talks about how she came to that decision.

I've been back and forth out of Ireland over the last eight years, just for short periods of time. On my seventeenth birthday, I decided I wanted to travel so I got my passport and a ticket and went over to Holland to find a job. But by law, you can't work under eighteen there and though I really tried, eventually I gave up. So I went back to Dublin, took the first job I could get that paid money, saved up every penny and went away again. I hitched with my boyfriend to France, Spain and over to Morocco and back to France for the grape season. We arrived early for the season, so the farmer gave us subs off our wages and a place to live out in the countryside, this little hut, where we cooked over a fire, so it was a really eventful summer.

I was a bit worried about my parents' reactions before I went. I had to get them to sign for my passport but they were more relaxed about it than I was. I got away with it – or I felt I'd gotten away with it. They've never enforced their will too much unless it's over someone going really crazy. I became a bit of a punk when I was fifteen and my parents didn't like the way I was dressing, they wouldn't let me out of the house and took my shoes so I couldn't get out and things like that ... so, I had to change my image!

I left school and got the first job I could, in a launderette close to where we were living. I got a flat over a shop and a part-time job there as well. I was only sixteen, I had two jobs, a cheap rent, life was busy and my friends all lived round the area. My parents didn't react too much to me leaving school so young. My Dad's a lecturer in a technical college but he never forced his will on us about the education we wanted. I made choices and that was that.

The reason I left home so young was mainly because I came from a large family and I wanted to just get out and assert myself more. We've twelve children altogether – seven brothers and four sisters and I was in the middle. This is shock horror for a protestant family! People presume you're a catholic family and that you don't believe in contraception. But that wasn't the reason. My parents liked children and having them. They weren't against contraception. I grew up in an atmosphere where what the Catholic Church professed wasn't relevant, we had our own ideas. It was very relaxed in that sense.

My family are Huguenot. My grandfather said we originally came from France, three or four generations ago. Initially, they were involved in the railways, that was their livelihood, but their children didn't continue that on, like my great-grandfather was a bookbinder. That's my father's family, who lived on the south side of Dublin. My mother came from the north side of the city. I don't know much about her side of the family – it's possibly Scottish in origin. My parents had something in common in that they were protestant, so they ended up mingling in the protestant circles and that's where they met, at some dance in Ranelagh.

My parents never went to church. We were encouraged to go, we'd always be brought along with an older brother or sister until we made the decision not to go, then that was it. I went to a protestant primary school so there you regarded yourself as fairly normal. You didn't think you were in a minority though if you come from a large family in a protestant school, then you're an outsider. In later years, with more knowledge, you'd realise that protestants were regarded as different in the South of Ireland. Even as a child, I was often shocked by what my friends, who were nearly all catholic, were telling me – we were sinners, we didn't go to church, or we could go to church when we wanted, so they were telling us that we were going to go to hell. You don't want to be an outsider as a child, you like to just blend in, so I remember thinking, 'I want to be a catholic.' Catholicism was interesting to you because you knew nothing about it, but later on, you'd be glad you'd escaped.

In teenage years, once people found out you were protestant you would often be disliked, and you had to try and work out for yourself why people were taking this attitude. Then, doing history in school, it never dawned on me, in the early years anyway, that protestants had come into Ireland, that they hadn't just always been there, that we were not liked because most protestants were of English descent. I had one catholic boyfriend. I remember him saying to me that if his friends knew of a protestant walking down the street, they would think of shooting them. The sad thing was this was the sort of attitude they would adopt towards protestants when I was growing up in Dublin. That was probably my first awareness of the differences. I was fourteen then. I thought about that for a long time. For many years I carried that image in my head of people's attitudes towards protestants. An image of hatred, a sense that I didn't belong. It always affected me and made me feel like I've been brought up in Ireland and yet I don't really belong here. But going away, I realise I don't belong anywhere else either. So in Ireland, I'll always be regarded as an outsider. Once I speak my name, they presume you're not of Irish descent. They just regard protestants as English. You become more cautious about letting people know your religion. You'd be more inclined to forget that you were baptised, even though you don't practise any religion. At the same time, you're still part of the country, what can you do?

The troubles breaking out in the North again certainly does heighten that awareness of the differences because it's nearly a religious war up in the North of Ireland and it's had repercussions in the South. People can't break away from the past really. The past is what shapes society today and even in England you get the attitude that they don't like the French and the French don't like the English – it's just been carried on.

After I'd worked in the launderette, I got a job in a shipping company, a good position that paid well but it was mainly protestant run. Even at the time, I realised that becaus I was protestant and because of the school I'd gone to, that had helped me get into the firm having left school early. I worked there for a while before I went travelling again. This time when I went back to Dublin, I decided I'd better get a career together of some sort and keep my feet

Rachel Harbron

on the ground for a while – that's what it felt like. I started on this cookery course which lasted two months. I enjoyed it and I got into the cookery itself. I would go to the library and get all sorts of books on cookery and nutrition, broadening my mind in that area. I was more interested in the foreign cookery because I felt like I was getting an insight into other countries, how they cooked and how they lived, so that kept my interest up. I read cookery books like people read novels. After that course, I'd done really well and it got me a job in the Powerscourt shopping centre. Then along came an opportunity to work in a new vegetarian restaurant. They had completely different theories on cookery and food – they were into macrobiotics and there was a whole philosophy that went with it. It gave me more awareness, more caring towards what I was cooking. I also went to college for the City & Guilds Catering Certificate. It's an international qualification so it's very useful. Apart from the education, I wanted the piece of paper at the end, just because if I wanted to travel, I didn't want to be discriminated against. I wanted to be able to assert myself. I know myself that you can know ten times more than people with qualifications, but at the same time, I saw people being put down because they hadn't got the qualifications. I didn't want that to happen to me.

When I finished college, I felt I'm free now, I've got the qualifications, I can go and travel. It was July of last year when I came to England, without a job when I left. I'd sent off CVs and I didn't really get much response but I felt there would always be something in the catering line. I had a sister who was married here and who was more than happy to have me come and stay with her. I felt very positive about coming to London, new people and experiences, a life away from family and friends, to see how I could be out there on my own, see what I could achieve. I also felt it would be an opportunity in my cookery career, because there were more options in London.

My sister and her husband collected me, and taking me home he was saying, 'Well, how long do you think you'll spend looking for a job?' 'I reckon a maximum of two weeks,' I said. 'No way,' he said, 'there's a lot of unemployment.' He didn't believe that it would be possible. But I felt really organised. I had my CVs all made out and clothes to wear to interviews. I was confident.

The first thing I did was to go to a job agency and they had a job starting the next day in an Italian restaurant. The people there were very nice, but they were used to male chefs in the kitchen, and they were just being too nice to me. They couldn't handle a woman in the kitchen at all, so I wasn't being allowed enough freedom. I would have been happier being treated equally. My second job I got after a week – it was a centralised bakery for a chain of wholefood restaurants. I'd various duties – baking bread, pizza section, pastry section, cooking section and churning out baps, bread rolls. So it was quite intense. The vans come in for the deliveries and you have to work fast to get everything boxed up and ready to go to get to the restaurants in time for early morning breakfast, then mid-morning cakes and lunches. You could be on any area and you had to get proficient in all areas. I picked it up pretty quickly because I was used to cookery so I'd be on a job for a day or two and I'd know it. But there's quite a high turnover of staff and often people would never have done catering at all, so you'd be training them in. You'd only be there a short while yourself and you'd be training in new people. It was quite demanding in that sense. It was physical but it didn't require too much of your mind and you were working with people from different countries, so you could discuss whatever you were into with them. It was interesting. The wages were the usual, subsistence.

I was working from six in the morning till one in the afternoon, straight shift, so I had to be up pretty early. The second month, I started cycling in. I felt safer cycling because I had met a few drunks travelling in on the tube at that hour and it made me a bit nervous. I enjoyed cycling because it was summer and it was nice to feel the sun on your face and I felt independent.

It's funny, you know, in Ireland I'm regarded as an outsider because I'm protestant and in England I felt really conscious that I was Irish. I was half afraid to open my mouth in front of people in case they'd say, 'Well, she's Irish and she's thick.' I was afraid to make a mistake in my new job, afraid people would think, 'Typical Irish.' I really had this thing in my head that the English think the Irish are stupid so in a way I was really nervous when I started. I'd say it took me about a month and all that month I felt unsure of myself and I felt, am I making the right decision or should I go home? I hadn't felt like that before. But I persisted and then I overcame my fears and became more confident. There were all nationalities working there and I was welcomed in and made to feel at ease. But it's a feeling I have, especially among upper middle-class English people, that they don't regard you in the same light as themselves. We are sort of second-class citizens, which you feel strongly. They might make jokes ragging your accent or whatever but the thought is still there, that in a general way they regard themselves as better. At the same time, I've met a lot of English people and have a lot of English friends as well. I don't really mix in Irish circles. I don't go in for giving yourself a separate identity like, 'We're Irish, let's all come together.' I like people to really intermix and not establish themselves as separate entities.

I've met quite a few Irish people over here that I knew in Dublin. It was amazing, I was only in London a couple of weeks when I walked into a bunch around Covent Garden and one of them had been my next-door neighbour! It often seems like the Irish government is glad to get rid of a few more people off the dole queues, that's what it's like. They're really glad if you decide that you're going to England – that's it, they've got a few more people off their shoulders. It's about time that they took an interest in the amount of emigrants from Ireland. There are so many, it's about time they recognised them.

I've never felt homesick, I've always felt really detached. I feel more that I belong outside Ireland for the time being. I love Ireland at the same time but I don't know whether I see myself going back there . . . not yet anyway. I can see myself working here trying to achieve something and travelling to experience other people's lives, other people's worlds.

Some time after this interview, Rachel left England to travel in China.

Second Generation Experience

You have to make a choice about who you are

Saturday music class at the Irish Centre, Camden

Below: Second generation Irish school girls and friends, outside their convent school
Bottom: Irish punks at a Pogues concert

Going to Mass on St Patrick's Day

Below: A christening in Whitechapel, East London
Bottom: Waiting to go on – A feis, 1985

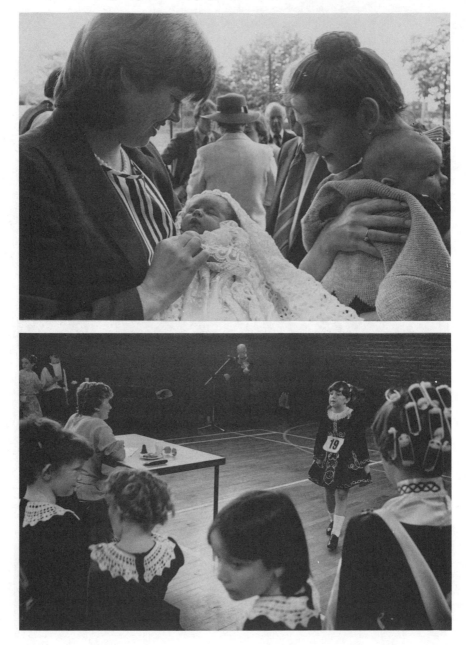

Glasgow Irish flute band members

Jenneba Sie Jalloh

In one of her poems, Jenneba Sie Jalloh describes herself as,

> 'a black woman, an African
> With an alternate Irish heartbeat'.

Here she focuses on her Irish heritage.

It's only now as I get older that I feel Irish, I feel my Irish blood. When I was a child, like most children, I just took things for granted, but my mum was always at the forefront, and my Irish background was always there. She's always talked to me, and told me about her experiences and her childhood in Ireland. It all seeped through to me, it all went into my subconscious.

My mum was born in Limerick, in a really small village. When she was five years old she moved with all her family to Dublin, to Cabra. Some of my relations in Ireland are still living there now.

My father's from Freetown, Sierra Leone. My grandmother is Creole, and my grandfather was from the Fulla tribe. They're a market tribe, shop keepers, things like that. When he was sixteen my father stowed away and came to Glasgow. He never went back after that, never visited Sierra Leone after that time. So he spent sixteen years in Freetown, and the rest of his life – he was fifty-two when he died – all around England, Scotland and Tiger Bay in Wales.

I was born in the centre of London, in Paddington Hospital. I'm an only child. My mum wanted a family for me, so I went every summer to Archway to stay with one of my aunts and cousins when they came over from Dublin. When I was seven I went to Brittas Bay in Wicklow for one summer. That was really good, we stayed in a caravan with my aunt and three cousins. The second time I went I was about fourteen, and I went on my own to stay with my aunt and cousins who used to come over here. But I always felt like an outsider. I think it wasn't only because I'm black, but also because I'm a Londoner, and they thought of me as English. I think I was kept away from the family in a lot of ways, obviously because my father's black and my mother's a bit of an outsider because of it. There was no contact between my dad and my mum's family.

As a child I really wanted my mother's family, because none of my father's family is here. Then at about the age of fourteen I decided I didn't want them any more, because I really felt that they didn't want me. Then last year I met all my cousins at a wedding. I went through traumas deciding whether or not to go. I thought to myself, after all these years do I really want to see them and relive the memories of childhood? I was scared of being with my mum where she would be part of the family, and maybe I wouldn't be. I was scared of losing her, just for that day. In fact, everybody was really nice to me. I'm glad I went though I was always aware of myself. One cousin actually asked me if I 'knew my father' which showed that they knew nothing about me and resorted to stereotypes. At fourteen that would have affected me, but at twenty-two I was prepared.

They're two great influences, the African and the Irish, but they both came in different ways. My father talked to me about Africa. His stories were wonderful. He used to tell me about smoking weed in the jungle, about the beach, about bunking off and sitting on the dock watching the ships going to England, and saying he wanted to go ... but they were just snippets of information. I remember having my ears pierced when I was six, because my grandmother was going to send me earrings and all African girls had their ears pierced. He always said to me 'You're African.' He called me Jenneba, when everybody else called me Jenny. The one thing I regret is that because my dad died when I was fourteen, I never spoke to him as an adult. Now I can speak to my mother woman to woman, but I never spoke to my father in that way. I can romanticise about my dad – when the African influence came, it came hard and strong. But if I was to be honest, the influence of my mum and the Irish heritage is a lot more profound, because it was constant. I was surrounded by Irish, hearing colloquialisms and my mother's accent. I was hearing things as I grew up, and it had a great influence on me in many ways, a more subtle influence.

My mum is republican, so I've always been brought up really strongly for a united Ireland. I was taught rebel songs – I used to sing them to people when they came round, things like that. I remember my mum telling me that her grandmother saw people dying on the road with grass in their mouths during the Famine, but I wasn't taught Irish history at school. I was taught it first at college, doing A levels. They said, 'We're now going to deal with "the Irish Problem".' I said, 'The Irish *problem*?' I questioned it, and that was the first time that I didn't like the way it was being put across. The second time, at the poly, we were doing literature and they said, 'We're doing English literature here, the poets and playwrights, Shaw and Oscar Wilde and Sheridan.' I said, 'Excuse me, I really don't think they're English.' We argued for about half an hour. The whole class was bored because I wouldn't let it drop. But I really felt indignant. It's a real English thing anyway, it's like what they do with black athletes. They claim who they want, when they want, when it serves their nationalism. But the thing is, those lecturers have been lecturing the same thing for years, they're not going to change it.

As a small child I had no conflict about my mum being white. She told me that when I was about four or five I said to her, 'Mummy, am I black?' She was taken aback by this and she said, 'Yes, yes, you are black.' She told my dad and my dad thought it was really funny. Later on, in school, the biggest thing for me was that my father was African rather than West Indian. My school was 80 per cent black and mainly West Indian. I used to say he was

American, because Africans were, you know, called monkeys and savages and cannibals and the rest of it. It's awful now, when I look back on it. It's all part of what the colonialists have left us.

My mum and dad never sat down and talked to me about racism and being mixed race. My dad would talk about Africa and say I was an African child. My mum would talk about Ireland and say that I'd get on because everyone would like me for what I am. With a lot of children of mixed race now, their parents consciously tell them. Looking back on it, I can remember feeling apart at primary school. There weren't very many black people, so my friends were white – funnily enough they were all catholics, but they were white English. I can remember feeling a bit different. Maybe when I was younger I put it down to other things, but I know I felt a bit like an outsider. I was about eighteen years old when I actually sat down and confronted it, and cried about it, and felt I didn't belong. My identity crisis came at eighteen, which is quite late, you know.

At school we learnt about the slave trade, we learnt that it was really bad, that it was really wrong, but we never learnt about how great the civilisations were in Africa, before the people were taken as slaves. So, although we were given a sympathetic view, we were given a really negative view. It wasn't put into perspective – they left out a very fundamental part that could have given a lot of black children a lot of pride, because to be taught that your history started at the time of slavery is pretty tragic.

My mother didn't really let me explore my African heritage as I was growing up, she didn't go into it as much as she could have done. Some younger white women now, being married to black men, take time and trouble to spell out the history to their children. But my mother came from a different generation. I think in a way she was a bit scared that she'd be losing me to my father. Many times, especially in my teenage years, I must have caused her so much agony. If I didn't get what I wanted I'd say, 'If I was white you'd have given it to me.' It must have really pained her – I know now that it did. She didn't want to hear about racism, because it caused her too much pain. It's really silly, because she knew through her own experience of being Irish in the 1950s, you know, 'No Blacks, No Irish, No Dogs'. Whenever there was a bomb scare, she used to say that she'd ask for her fare in a really low voice 'cause she didn't want them to know that she was Irish – it used to pain me inside to think of it. So, from somebody who's had those same experiences I've always found it really odd that she didn't want to accept it for black people. The reason is that she didn't want to accept it for *me*. It's me who's made her aware – well she's been aware, but it's me who's actually made her come to terms and face it, that black people are discriminated against.

I think you can only condemn a person for thinking things that may be racist or sexist if, after you've told them or you've made them aware, they still believe those things. I've argued with my mum about things, and then, with other people she'll make all the points that I've made in our arguments! I took her to the Irish Women's Centre when I was doing the poetry reading and some women said to me, 'Why do you think of yourself as black and not Irish?' I was just about to reply, when my mum stood up in front of me and said, 'Well, obviously . . .', and she took over. I didn't get a word in edgeways, and she was arguing with these women about why I see myself as black, you know. And it was a lovely thing to hear as well, I was really proud of her.

When I read my mum the poem I wrote to her, she just cried. Part of that poem said:

> To break the bond
>   And tell the person from whose womb you came,
> That your struggle is a different one
>   Your fight a different fight
> Where you go, they can't follow,
>   They must remain outside
> And let you fight for what's rightfully yours
>   Away from their love and their guiding light.
>
> How different are we?
>   Are we as different as they say?
> I hear all round me that it is
>   The white man, the white oppressor,
> Who is keeping me down.
>
> But when I need that love,
>   That guiding light,
> That heart in tune with mine,
>   Who can I turn to but my Mother,
> That person whose skin colour is different to mine.

She cried, and she said, 'I shouldn't have had you.' But I tried to explain that you can't say things like that. I'm trying to be a realist. I know there are things we can't relate on because she is white, but that could be the same for anybody whose mother or father is from a different culture. There's a bond between my mother and myself that could never be equalled and could never be surpassed.

I've had to deal with racism from my own flesh and blood. What really struck me once was my aunt actually sounding quite bitter about black people standing up and, you know, protesting. She said what I think maybe other Irish people living in London say, 'We went through it, and we never made all that fuss and nonsense. We got on with it.' What she hears is that black people have got equal this and equal that, and that you have to give certain jobs to black people, which of course, isn't true. So, she says, 'We don't have any of that.' And there's a kind of bitterness. It's a kind of jealousy in a way. It could be partly because Irish people are white people. It could be that when people are together under the same oppression, some want to stay apart and think they'll get on better if they don't meet other people who are oppressed. Some black people feel like that too. But I feel more hurt by Irish people being racist, because I am a part of them.

As a black person of mixed race, you are always fighting to say 'I am black', and sometimes it can be a bit difficult to bring in another part of your background, especially if it is white. For me, I am part of my Irish heritage. I am stirred by Irish music, by the haunting pipes; I'm proud of the history of struggle and the resistance to British imperialist forces; I want to see Ireland united as a socialist republic; I can visualise the wild countryside, and when I hear Irish people, or something about Ireland on telly, my ears do prick up straight away, same as if I hear black. If I hear anti-Irish jokes, I *always* say something – people moan about that. I was really proud and excited to read my poetry at the Irish Women's Centre. I've never, ever attempted to deny any part of my heritage, African or Irish. But there are people in the Irish community, and in the Black community, who would want to rob me of my identity. I've been told 'you're black', 'you're white', 'half-caste', I'm this, that and the other. I'm not denying any part of my heritage by stating what I am. I'm not white, I'm black. I'm part Irish, part African. I call myself an African woman with an Irish mother, and a Londoner. I want to pass on whatever I've got to my children, so I've got to work it out for myself. So, for those people who want to deny me, well, I think it's them who've got the problem, not me.

Yvonne Hayes describes growing up Irish in London in the 1970s.

W hen I was sixteen I was a punk and it was the fashion then to sew a Union Jack on to your jeans. My parents went mad, that was what made me do it actually. But I remember one day I was out with my friends and I was sitting there looking at this Union Jack thinking, 'Why have I got this on my jeans? What's this thing doing on my leg?' – so I went home and ripped it off and I got a little tricolour flag and I sewed that on. I thought if it's fashion to have a flag on your leg, at least I'll have my own flag on my leg.

At that age, although I always knew I was Irish, there was a complete gap between the sense of Irishness within the Irish community and any other way of being Irish. Y'know, I couldn't have been a punk and going to a céili or anything like that, and I didn't want to then either because I think that part of growing up is that you start doing different things. As a child, your Irishness is connected to your parents and that's quite a traditional way and all of a sudden, when you're an adolescent, you have to go the other way – you have to go the 'English' way to express yourself because you can't do it the Irish way. You'd be shaming everyone! At about twelve, I started going to discos and getting involved with English sorts of things, so from twelve to sixteen there was nothing Irish there really, nothing Irish in anything I was doing. I think it was just a lack of identity because I wasn't English either. I didn't feel English, though all through that time my parents accused me of being English. 'You're really getting into the English way of life,' they'd say. They thought that would be the biggest insult and would stop me doing it.

Because my parents were Irish and catholic, they were a hell of a lot stricter on me than the parents of a lot of people I was mixing with. They were allowed much more freedom. I think that was also to do with both my parents coming from small towns where the whole town was like their mother. Suddenly they've a young daughter in London, and I'm the only girl, and they just don't think you can take care of yourself. Whereas I was brought up here. For them, it's a more frightening place than I'd find it. As well as that, I think maybe male and female stereotypes are a bit stronger in Irish families – the boys go out playing football and the girls stay in and help Mum to lay the table. Although I think that's a woman's problem no matter where you come from, I think it's a bit stronger in Irish families. The catholic influence too means you've got to be very good and pure ... a good girl.

When I came out of that phase, it was because of politics and what was happening in Northern Ireland. All of a sudden, I had to make a choice about what I thought about it all, and I decided it was a lot more important than what I'd been doing. I think that was what pulled me through the other side. I don't know if it was any one particular thing which struck me, or if it was just that things had been brewing up in me for a while that I had tried to ignore. It meant being openly Irish – not that I was ever under cover Irish – but talking to people about things and going out of my way to find out what was going on and seeing if there was anything I could do ... supporting demonstrations or things like that.

You have to make a choice about who you are. If you look at the National Front, there are kids in it who have got Irish surnames. I'm sure a lot of them are born to Irish parents and must have gone through these changes like me, but they come out of this phase in the end having completely lost their identity and just being English. They get involved in the National Front through being skinheads at that adolescent stage, and the leaders of some of these skinhead groups are Nazis and these kids get caught up in this. Perhaps anti-Irish feeling and jokes make them feel bad about their identity – but whether they identify as Irish or not, they're white. Maybe being anti-black seems like an answer if they want to build themselves up. But then, to be in the National Front you could end up hating Irish people as well, and not identifying with them.

It annoys me that a lot of Irish people I know in Kilburn will come out and talk about racism against Irish people, and be very good about that, but they'll say something racist about black people. When you have an argument with them about it, or discuss it with them, they don't like that. They start accusing you of not being really Irish. If you say, for instance, that black people have as much right as Irish people to jobs and council houses, then you're accused of being anti-Irish. It's their last tactic to have a go at you ... They'll start accusing me of being anti-Irish because I'll stick up for black people. That I find really annoying. It really gets my back up. Their proudness to be Irish is a purely nationalist thing. They'll accept you are Irish until you disagree with them about racism and that's quite a problem I think ... and I haven't worked out how to deal with that yet.

As a child, I always thought of myself as Irish. We were an Irish home like. My aunts and cousins lived near and we always went back to Ireland for a holiday, when we could afford it. There were often stories about the 'boys in the mountains' and bringing food up to them ... maybe in the War of Independence. These stories would always be in the background though they were never given that much importance because my parents tried to fit in with things over here, just tried to keep their heads down and not get into trouble. I think they felt like that because when they came over here there was anti-Irish feeling towards them. For Irish people, there's nothing else that distinguishes them from being English, as long as they keep their mouths shut. And if you are trying to bring up a family and build a home, you just try and fit in with the establishment and don't put yourself out on a limb too much, so you don't get into trouble.

My mum came over just after the war. She was working as a nanny and she got really ill. She was working in a house where they were really mean. They wouldn't give her enough food or heating and she developed pleurisy and they still didn't look after her. She was made to carry on working so it got worse and worse and developed into pneumonia and TB. She was given a fifty-fifty chance of survival. A lot of Irish women who did domestic work had very bad conditions and were treated badly by their employers. She talks a lot about that, and that kind of anti-Irish feeling comes up now and again when my parents are talking, but a lot of the time they try and pretend it didn't happen.

I think at one stage we were the only Irish family living in our street – so that set us apart a bit. We all went to Catechism on a Saturday and Mass on a Sunday, as a family. It was obvious where we were going and with things like my brothers' First Communion and my First Communion, I mean, you couldn't miss us. Of course, the Church was a social thing for us too. Catechism wasn't just for going and learning catechism, it was for meeting friends. And then after church on Sunday, if you went to twelve o'clock Mass, you'd go into the social club and you'd meet people there. It was also about the only day in the week that my mum could go out, 'cause the rest of the time she'd be in with us. But once a week, she could go up the social club and meet people and the majority of the people up there would be Irish. It'd be quite a good social scene.

I think the religious side was very important to my parents as well. They wanted us to grow up catholics. Y'know, they had faith and believed in God, but I think even more so the cultural part of it was important, because when I didn't want to go to Mass and wouldn't go, they were always on at me and most of it was, 'Oh, Irish people died to keep this religion going and I'd hate to be the first in my family that ever rejected my faith . . .' For them, there was no separation between being Irish and being catholic. But to me, being Irish meant more than just going to church and knowing Irish people, so there was that difference. Maybe my parents felt it was a grip on their background in this country, that their grip on their Irishness was the Church. I don't think I ever felt I had to be catholic to be Irish.

I was proud of being Irish. I remember in my first year at primary school, I must have been four or five, the first teacher we had was really good. She used to make children feel really proud of their background – she was always encouraging me and other kids who were other nationalities. But then as we went further on into primary school, some bad feeling did arise from other teachers, I remember that. We had to do projects on different countries once, but the way that the teacher was telling people about Ireland was ridiculous . . . Irish people running round in bogs! She thought it was very funny to bring out anti-Irish jokes as well. It made me feel really bad and really stupid, because she was the teacher and she was telling my friends that Irish people were a bit kind of subnormal and yet they knew I was Irish, so it made me feel quite intimidated, I suppose.

I think the turning point came when, in primary school, a lad came in, straight over from Ireland, and he was treated terrible because he used to put

220

his hand up and say 'sir', like he did in Ireland, I suppose. But the two of us combined together and y'know it was quite good then. One time, the whole school was going to the RAF museum in Hendon, it was the Queen who opened it, and we were all to go down with Union Jacks and wave at her. Well, me and Stephen wouldn't go and we were the only ones out of our year who didn't want to see the Queen. The teachers were a bit shocked and said, 'Well, you'll have to stay in and do work then!' So we said, 'OK.' I didn't tell my parents, I don't think they would have liked it very much. Inwardly they might have thought it was quite good, but outwardly they would've said it was bad and all that.

The secondary school I went to was a catholic grammar school. My three brothers had gone to grammar schools so my mum said, 'You're the only girl and you've got to go to a grammar school because otherwise, your brothers will think they're better than you.' But it was me as well. I wanted to go to a catholic school. I was only eleven, and I think I had this glamorous image of wandering around saying, 'Yes, Sister', and being really good – which wasn't me at all, because I was never a good kid. I'd watched that film about St Bernadette that had been on the telly, and I just thought, oh yeah, I'd really like to be like that, she's so sweet and innocent, so I thought, I'll go to a catholic school. The school I'd gone to before had down-to-earth working-class people, but this new school was quite an upper middle-class kind of school. There was quite a lot of Irish kids but many of them didn't even know they were Irish and that was quite annoying. I remember walking home with a girl one day – she was about thirteen at the time – and there was graffiti up on the walls like, 'IRA' and she said, 'Oh, IRA, is that the English or the Irish lot?' And she was Irish!

There was never any Irish evening or anything like that at the school. I think that would have been important because, as I say, some people didn't even know they were Irish there and I think that's pretty sad. If you have that culture behind you, you've got to keep a grip on who you are, and you've got to keep things alive. I wanted to learn the fiddle at school because there was this really talented girl in my class and I wanted to be able to play like she did. So, I told this teacher exactly what I wanted to do and she signed me up for the viola and actually made me try and learn all this classical stuff. I tried to explain that it really wasn't what I wanted to learn, but she thought I was really bad for not wanting to learn it. But I mean, my classical music was Irish traditional music and why shouldn't I have been allowed to learn that?

I went back on holidays to Ireland regularly, mainly to my mum's place. I remember the journeys over. We always seemed to be out on deck. All the seats inside used to be taken and with second-class seats, they never had enough of them for the passengers. I can remember sitting on them really uncomfortable slatted wooden benches, at three o'clock in the morning and the boat going up and down, waves coming over and being sick into a polythene bag. Terrible. I hated that, but then I remember being in Ireland

and on the train, and day'd start breaking and looking out the window and thinking, 'Oh, Ireland, and it's all green fields and everything.' I used to really love that; it was a sort of euphoric feeling.

My mother's home town was very small then. It's on the coast and mountainous with a river running through it. When I was a kid it was amazing, because you know in London you're taught not to talk to strangers and to keep walking straight ahead ... and then suddenly in Ireland, everyone's saying hello to you all over the place everybody knows you. I'd be walking down the street on my own and people'd come up and say, 'Oh, you're so-and-so's daughter' and buy me ice-creams.

I think they saw me as Irish until the last time I went back. I had had a gap of about six years, the town had grown a bit and there were people there I didn't know. I had to explain to them then that I was Irish and they'd say, 'But how can you be Irish, you were born and brought up in England?' It doesn't annoy me when people just ask 'cause that's fair enough as I've got an English accent, but I hate it when you have to start explaining everything. I think I said to someone, if I was born on a boat coming over, it wouldn't make me a fish, would it?

Where you happen to be born doesn't make you what you are. Everything about me is Irish, my background, my people, everything, and that's what I feel I am. I'm Irish.

Index